Brain-Powered Lessons to Engage All Learners

Author
LaVonna Roth, M.S.Ed.

SHELL EDUCATION

Publishing Credits

Robin Erickson, *Production Director*; Lee Aucoin, *Creative Director*;
Timothy J. Bradley, *Illustration Manager*; Emily R. Smith, M.A.Ed., *Editorial Director*;
Jennifer Wilson, *Editor*; Evelyn Garcia, M.A.Ed., *Editor*; Amber Goff, *Editorial Assistant*;
Grace Alba Le, *Designer*; Corinne Burton, M.A.Ed., *Publisher*

Image Credits

p. 87, bortonia/iStockphoto, zaricm/iStockphoto; p. 88, girlfrommars/iStockphoto, dumayne/iStockphoto;
p. 89, yayayoyo/iStockphoto; all other images Shutterstock

Standards

© 2004 Mid-continent Research for Education and Learning (McREL)
© 2007 Teachers of English to Speakers of Other Languages, Inc. (TESOL)
© 2007 Board of Regents of the University of Wisconsin System. World-Class Instructional Design and Assessment (WIDA)
© 2010 National Governors Association Center for Best Practices and Council of Chief State School Officers (CCSS)

Shell Education
5301 Oceanus Drive
Huntington Beach, CA 92649-1030
http://www.shelleducation.com
ISBN 978-1-4258-1184-6
© 2014 Shell Educational Publishing, Inc.

Table of Contents

Table of Contents *(cont.)*

A Letter To You

Dear Educator,

I want to take a moment to thank you for the inspiration that you are! As more mandates fall upon your shoulders and changes are made, I admire your drive, passion, and willingness to keep putting our students first. Every decision we make as educators should come down to one simple question: "Is this decision in the best interest of our students?" This reflects not our opinion, our philosophy, or our own agenda, but simply what is going to make the greatest impact on our students in preparing them for life and career.

As you continue to be the best you can be, I want you to take a few moments each day, look in the mirror, and smile. Come on—I know you can give me a bigger smile than that! Go for the big Cheshire Cat smile with all teeth showing. Why? Because you are sometimes your greatest cheerleader. Now, take that same smile and pass it on to colleagues, students, and parents. Attitude is catching—so let's share the one that puts smiles on others' faces! You will feel better and your day will be better.

Now, tear out this page. Tape it to a place where you will see it every... single... day. Yep! Tear it out. Tape it to the bathroom mirror, your dashboard, your desk—wherever you are sure to see it. Recite and do the following every single day—no joke:

I am appreciated!

I am amazing!

I am the difference!

From one educator to another, thank you for all you do!

—LaVonna Roth

P.S. Be sure to connect with me on social media! I would love to hear from you on these strategies and lessons.

About the Author

LaVonna Roth, M.S.Ed., is an international author, speaker, and consultant. She has had the privilege of working with teachers on three continents, sharing her passion for education and how the brain learns. Her desire to keep the passion of engaging instructional delivery is evident in her ideas, presentations, workshops, and books.

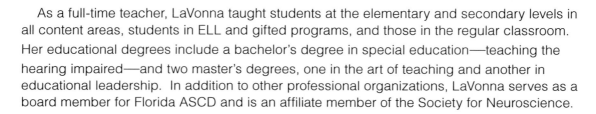

LaVonna has the unique ability to teach some of the more challenging concepts in education and make them simple and doable. Her goal is for teachers to be reenergized, to experience ideas that are practical and applicable, and have a great impact on student achievement because of the effect these strategies have on how the brain learns.

As a full-time teacher, LaVonna taught students at the elementary and secondary levels in all content areas, students in ELL and gifted programs, and those in the regular classroom. Her educational degrees include a bachelor's degree in special education—teaching the hearing impaired—and two master's degrees, one in the art of teaching and another in educational leadership. In addition to other professional organizations, LaVonna serves as a board member for Florida ASCD and is an affiliate member of the Society for Neuroscience.

As an author, she has written a powerful resource notebook, *Brain-Powered Lessons to Engage All Learners*, and is a dynamic and engaging presenter.

When LaVonna isn't traveling and speaking, she relaxes by spending time with her family in the Tampa, Florida area. She is dedicated to putting students first and supporting teachers to be the best they can be.

Acknowledgements

My family
My friends
All educators
Teacher Created Materials staff

I believe we accomplish great things when we surround ourselves with great people and take action. Thank you for all you do!

—LaVonna Roth

The Power of the Brain

"What actually changes in the brain are the strengths of the connections of neurons that are engaged together, moment by moment, in time."

—Dr. Michael Merzenich

The brain is a very powerful organ, one we do not completely understand or know everything about. Yet science reveals more and more to us each day.

As educators, we have a duty to understand how the brain learns so that we can best teach our students. If we do not have an understanding of some of the powerful tools that can help facilitate our teaching and allow us to better target the brain and learning, we lose a lot of time with our students that could be used to serve them better. Plus, the likelihood of doing as much reteaching will lessen.

This is where *Brain-Powered Lessons to Engage All Learners* comes in! The eight strategies included within the lessons are designed around how the brain learns as a foundation. In addition, they are meant to be used as a formative assessment, include higher-order thinking, increase the level of engagement in learning, and support differentiation. For detailed information on each strategy, see pages 12–19.

What Makes the Brain Learn Best

As you explore the strategies in this book, keep the following key ideas in mind.

The content being taught and learned must:

◎ be engaging

◎ be relevant

◎ make sense

◎ make meaning

◎ involve movement

◎ support memory retention

The Power of the Brain *(cont.)*

Be Engaging

In order for students to pay attention, we must engage the brain. This is the overarching theme to the rest of the elements. Too often, students are learning complacently. Just because students are staring at the teacher, with pencil in hand and taking notes, does not mean they are engaged. For example, we know that they are engaged when they answer questions or are interacting with the information independently with a teacher or another student. We don't always know when they are engaged just by looking at them. Sometimes, it's a simple question or observation of what they are doing that helps identify this. Body language can tell us a lot, but do not rely on this as the only point of observation. Many teachers may have not gone into teaching to "entertain," but entertaining is one component of engaging. As neuroscience research has revealed, it was noted as early as 1762 that the brain does change (neuroplasticity) based on experiences (Doidge 2007). It rewires itself based upon experiences and new situations, creating new neural pathways. "Even simple brain exercises such as presenting oneself with challenging intellectual environments, interacting in social situations, or getting involved in physical activities will boost the general growth of connections" (HOPES 2010, §2). This is fantastic if we are creating an environment and lessons that are positive and planned in a way that fires more neurons that increase accurate learning.

> **"Even simple brain exercises such as presenting oneself with challenging intellectual environments, interacting in social situations, or getting involved in physical activities will boost the general growth of connections"** (HOPES 2010, §2).

The Power of the Brain *(cont.)*

As a reflection for you, think about the following with respect to student engagement:

◎ What are the students doing during the lesson? Are they doing something with the information that shows they are into it? Are they asking questions? Are they answering?

◎ What is their body language showing? Are they slumped, or are they sitting in a more alert position? Are their eyes glazed and half-closed, or are they bright, alert, and paying attention to where their focus should be?

◎ Who is doing most of the talking and thinking? Move away from being the sage on the stage! Let the students be the stars. Share your knowledge with them in increments, but permit them to interact or explore.

◎ What could you turn over to students to have them create a way to remember the content or ask questions they have? What could be done to change up the lessons so they are interacting or standing? Yes, parts of lessons can be taught by having students stand for a minute or so. Before they sit, have them stretch or high-five a few classmates to break up the monotony.

Be Relevant

Why should the brain want to learn and remember something that has no relevance to us? If we want our students to learn information, it is important that we do what we can to make the information relevant. An easy way to achieve this is by bringing in some background knowledge that students have about the topic or making a personal connection. This does not need to take long.

As you will note, the lessons in this book start out with modeling. Modeling allows learners to have an understanding of the strategy and it also takes a moment to bring in what they know and, when possible, to make a personal connection. Consider asking students what they know about a topic and have them offer ideas. Or ask them to reflect on a piece of literature that you read or to ponder a question you have provided. For English language learners, this strategy is particularly effective when they can relate it to something of which they have a foundational concept and can make a connection to what they are learning. The language will come.

Make Sense

Is what you are teaching something that makes sense to students? Do they see the bigger picture or context? If students are making sense of what they are learning, a greater chance of it moving from working memory to long-term memory will increase. Some students can be asked if the idea makes sense and if they clearly understand. If they are able to explain it in their own words, they probably have a good grasp on metacognition and where they are in their learning. Other students may need to be coached to retell you what they just learned.

The Power of the Brain *(cont.)*

Make Meaning

Once students have had an opportunity to make sense of what they are learning, provide an opportunity for them to make meaning. This means that they have a chance to apply what was learned and actually "play" with the skills or concepts. Are they able to complete some tasks or provide questions on their own? Are they ready to take the information to higher levels that demonstrate the depth of understanding? (Refer to Webb's Depth of Knowledge for some additional insight into various levels of making meaning on pages 22–23.) For some students, simply asking a few questions related to what is being taught or having them write a reflection of what was just explained will allow you to check in on their understanding to see where they are before taking their thinking to a higher or a deeper level.

Involve Movement

This one is particularly important because of the plethora of research on movement. Dr. John Ratey wrote the book *Spark*, which documents how student achievement soars based on some changes made to students' physical education program in which students achieved their target heart-rate zone during their physical education time. Movement, particularly exercise, increases brain-derived neurotrophic factors (BDNF) that increase learning and memory (Vaynman, Ying, and Gomez-Pinilla 2004).

Knowing that getting students to achieve their target heart rate zone is not always an option, do what you can. Have students take some brain breaks that heighten their heart rate—even if for just a minute.

Movement has strong retention implications in other ways. Students can create a gesture connected to the lesson concept, or they can stand and move while they make meaning from what they learned. Movement is multisensory, thus, various regions of the brain are activated. When multiple brain pathways are stimulated, they are more likely to enter long-term potentiation from activating episodic and semantic memories.

If you come across a model lesson in this book in which not much movement is shared, or you find your students have been sitting longer than you may wish (you will know because their body language will tell you—unfortunately, we should have had them moving before this point), my challenge to you is to think of what movement you can add to the lesson. It could involve a gesture, a manipulative, or physically getting up and moving. If you are concerned about them calming back down, set your expectations and stick to them. Keep in mind that often when students "go crazy" when permitted to move, it's probably because they *finally* get to move. Try simple techniques to bring students back into focus. "Part of the process of assisting children in developing necessary skills is getting to the root of why they behave as they do" (Harris and Goldberg 2012, xiv).

The Power of the Brain *(cont.)*

Support Memory Retention

If we want our students to retain what we teach them, then it is important that we keep in mind what causes our brains to retain that information.

Key Elements to Memory Retention	Why
Emotions	We can create an episodic memory when we connect emotions to our learning.
Repetition	Repetition increases memory as long as there is engagement involved. Worksheets and drill and kill do not serve long-term memory well.
Patterns/Organization	When our brains take in messages, they begin to file the information by organizing it into categories.
Personal connection	Linking learning to one's self is a powerful brain tool for memory. This, too, can be tied to emotion, making an even stronger connection.
Linking new and prior knowledge	Taking in new information automatically results in connecting past knowledge to what is new.

(Roth 2012)

As you explore the strategies and lessons throughout this book, note how many of them incorporate the keys to memory retention and what engages our students' brains. As you begin to explore the use of these strategies on your own, be sure to keep the framework of those important components.

The bottom line—explore, have fun, and ask your students how they feel about lessons taught. They will tell you if they found the lesson interesting, engaging, and relevant. So get in there, dig in, and have some fun with your students while trying out these strategies and lessons!

Sort It
Strategy Overview

As our brains take in information, we immediately connect it to something known and begin filing it accordingly (Willis 2008). Each lobe of the brain takes responsibility for different information that is transferred across regions by a massive neural system that would put social networks out of business. The corpus callosum, connecting both hemispheres, assists in the networking, allowing the two hemispheres to interact and help each other out (Vermillion 2010). Sousa (2006) explains that the brain evaluates new stimuli for clues to help connect incoming information with stored patterns, categories of data, or past experiences, thereby extending existing patterns with the new input. Once the sensory input reaches the hippocampus, it is ready to fuse into memory (Eldridge et al. 2010). This fusion, however, can only occur if the prior knowledge in stored memory is first activated and sent to the hippocampus to connect with the new information.

Strategy Insight

In the *Sort It* strategy, students look for patterns, trends, or common themes as they sort through information and move around at the same time. Movement increases oxygen levels in the brain, which improves attention and leads to engagement. We are in a better position to learn when we move (Sousa 2006). In addition, the brain thrives on making predictions. Students predict where they think they fit and why. This is an important step in the learning process. Being wrong and being right helps our brain lock in on the learning. Either we are right and the brain celebrates with a burst of dopamine (pleasure) or we correct our thinking and the brain takes note of the correction because it wants to be right. This strategy allows students to make predictions about the topic of study and then explain their thinking. Students will have the opportunity to tap into their thinking, which provides the teacher an insight into where to make a correction or to celebrate their connection.

Throughout this process, students interact with the content while taking their thinking to a higher level. They physically move while looking at other students' cards and determine where they belong. During this process, they have already begun to predict as to what category they belong, and as they walk around, they confirm or shift their thinking based on what they see. Since there is the possibility of more than one answer, students can analyze and rearrange their original thoughts to justify the choices they make.

Teacher Notes

◎ Differentiate by giving easier words or concepts to students who are struggling. **Note:** We often underestimate the ability of a student. Let them struggle some so they learn, but not so much that they become frustrated.

◎ During the mingle part of the strategy, tell students to work with various students and not the same people each time.

It Takes Two
Strategy Overview

In this strategy, students compare and contrast two topics (e.g., stories, historical figures, types of clouds and shapes) using a T-chart and sticky notes. The goal is for students to analyze each topic and create a chart that represents their thinking. Thereafter, another group of students will evaluate whether it agrees with the original group's thoughts or, if not, if it is going to propose another way to think about the topic. The goal is for students to be able to think at a higher level by justifying either what each sticky note says and where each one is placed or if it qualifies to be on the T-chart at all.

Strategy Insight

Organization and thinking critically are key components in this strategy. Since we organize ideas in our brains systematically and create a neural pathway as more modalities are used, students increase their learning by seeing the information, sorting through what is important, organizing the facts by what is similar and what is different, and adding another level of value through student interaction (Van Tassell 2004). Each of these components plays an integral part in student engagement and retention (Covington 2000). It is another way for students to work with content at a level that is minds-on and hands-on.

Using sticky notes during this activity is important (as opposed to recording the similarities and differences on a sheet) because students' thinking will shift as they discuss and learn more. The sticky notes allow the graphic organizer to become manipulative, and it is a new way for them to see if they agree or disagree with their classmates and adjust accordingly.

Teacher Notes

◎ It is imperative that teachers observe during all stages of the lesson. This provides the feedback we need to determine the next direction of instruction. In addition, it allows an opportunity to guide students in their thinking, as some may struggle with concepts at a higher level. **Note:** Do not guide too much. A large part of learning is struggling through the process with a small amount of frustration but not so much that students give up.

◎ During discussions, students will likely discover that there can be more than one answer. That is where collaboration and cooperation pay off.

◎ For younger students, reconvene as a whole group and model the evaluation steps, using one group's chart.

Kinesthetic Word Webs
Strategy Overview

Movement is crucial to learning. We must move because the "sit-and-get" method is overused and not as effective as when we have the chance to increase our oxygen intake and shift the activity. Although there is no exact science as to the number of minutes that elapse before we should move or change direction, no more than 20 minutes is an adequate amount of time for learning to occur before we do something with what was learned (Schenck 2005). Our working memory can only hold so much information before it becomes fatigued or bored (Sousa 2006). Thus, implementing the suggested 20-minute time frame into teaching should help teachers to remember the importance of chunking material and allowing time for the brain to process material being learned.

We know what a web is on paper, but what is a Kinesthetic Word Web? It is a strategy that gets students up and moving with the content of the lessons. Picture a word web on paper. Now, turn the outer ovals on the word web into students and imagine their arms touching the person's shoulder in the center oval. That is a Kinesthetic Word Web.

Strategy Insight

The *Kinesthetic Word Webs* strategy is designed to take a paper-and-pencil activity and add movement and challenge to raise the level of engagement. As Wolfe and Brandt (1998) state, "The brain likes a challenge!" It seeks patterns. Patterns are required during this strategy in order to be successful.

Teacher Notes

◎ Be sure every student has a card. Do not worry about every student fitting into a word web. If a student cannot be a part of a Kinesthetic Word Web because his or her word has already appeared in the web or because there was not an exact number of students for each set, they can explain where they would go and why.

◎ **Note:** Some students do not like to be touched, so knowing students and their backgrounds is very important. As an alternative, they can each place a fist on a hip and connect elbow to elbow; they can extend a leg and touch foot to foot; or you can provide 15 inches of string to each student with the center student holding one end of all the strings.

Matchmaker
Strategy Overview

The importance of movement and having students get up out of their seats cannot be emphasized enough. Thus, here is another strategy that allows our students to do so. *Matchmaker* also provides students an opportunity to get repeated practice in an environment in which the repetition is guided and correct. This means that when students practice repeatedly, the likelihood of recall increases. A key factor here is that it must be correct practice. When students do this activity with one another, they are getting a chance to see repeated practice with automatic feedback provided about whether they are correct or not.

Strategy Insight

Every student is given an address label to wear. Each label is a vocabulary word, a concept, a formula, etc. On index cards are the matching definitions, illustrations, examples, synonyms, etc.

Students wear the address labels and stand in a circle with the index cards on the floor in the middle. Students hold hands and bend down to pick up an index card with their connected hands. Without letting go, they have to get the card they picked up to the correct person, according to his or her address label. This strategy can be repeated as many times as you wish to help students practice.

Teacher Notes

◎ An alternative to this is for students to not hold hands when they pick up a card. However, energy and engagement increase with the added challenge of holding hands and not letting go.

◎ Be sure to listen in and encourage students to discuss disagreements or to have them respond to a reason why a particular card goes with another card.

Reverse, Reverse!
Strategy Overview

Reverse, Reverse! is meant to be a challenging strategy. When students are under stress, there will often be not only a chemical but a physical change in the brain. Students must learn the skills to deal with stress, but in a safe and friendly environment. In this strategy, students will practice the speed and fluency of facts, but they will do so under pressure—a pressure that you can adjust or increase, depending upon the topic and age level of your students.

Strategy Insight

Students sit or stand in a circle. They are given a topic and asked to brainstorm what they know about it. One student begins by sharing a fact about the topic. Going clockwise, the next student must quickly say another fact related to the one just stated. If the student pauses more than five seconds or states an incorrect fact, the student that just finished must state the next fact (reversing the direction of participation). One student sits out to judge the facts and make sure rules are followed. Continue until participation stalls. For example, a math activity using this strategy can include counting by threes. The first student says, "3;" the next student says, "6;" the next says, "9." If the following student says, "13," the rotation reverses to the previous student, who must say, "Reverse," and must also say the correct answer, "12." The responses are now going counterclockwise. An example of using this strategy in social studies can include the three branches of government. The first student might say, "Legislative branch;" the second says, "Makes the laws;" the third student says, "Congress;" and the fourth says, "Checks and balances." The judge (student sitting out) can halt the flow to ask how the response relates to a previously said fact. If justified, the round continues. *Reverse, Reverse!* continues until a predetermined amount of clock time or number of times around the circle has been met.

Teacher Notes

◎ It is important to set the stage for students to feel safe when using this strategy. You may wish to take out the reverse portion at first and work on just the speed. Add the extra layer of difficulty for novelty and time-pressured practice.

◎ For younger students, you may choose to not have the next student say, "Reverse," but instead state the correct fact.

Show It with Dough!
Strategy Overview

Our brains recall pictures quite well. This phenomenon is called the *Pictorial Superiority Effect* (PSE) (Medina 2008). Simply put, the brain grasps pictures and can recognize and recall a picture with far less effort than it takes to recall text.

Through the use of dough sculptures, students think about a concept and make a three-dimensional representation, often moving from abstract to concrete ideas. This is a higher-level skill since it requires extended thinking to represent something in a new way (Bloom 1956).

Strategy Insight

Many concepts we teach are quite abstract, particularly as students progress in grade levels. This strategy often requires students to visualize the concept on a concrete level rather than an abstract level. Thus, this strategy is at a higher level because students are being asked to demonstrate their learning in a new way. Additionally, we are asking students to connect their visual representations to what they already know; therefore, we also incorporate activating prior knowledge and experiences, which in turn ties into something personal. This strategy can also impact other content areas and allows students the opportunity to use their creativity in an expressive way.

Teacher Notes

◎ Walk around as students create their sculptures and ask them to think about what they are making and why. Consider doing this very quietly so others do not hear what they are creating or use written communication.

◎ Place student sculptures on cardboard so they are easy to move or display.

◎ After students add more detail to their sculptures and write their stories, display them where others can enjoy them.

I'm in the Pic
Strategy Overview

I'm in the Pic is a strategy that targets various modalities for storage of memory in the brain. The more students can experience this strategy the better, because each of our senses is stored in different regions of the brain (Medina 2008). The way we learn the information dictates where much of the memory is stored and connected.

We can compare using our senses and experiences to when you learned how to ride a bike. Try to recall the approximate time of day and location of that first bike-riding experience. This is called *episodic memory*, as it refers to an event (or an episode) in your life (Sousa 2006; Sprenger 1999). Your episodic memory deals with time and location. Now, let us add emotion to this memory. As you learned to ride, you experienced movement and wind blowing in your face.

However, providing actual sensory experiences for all content is not always possible. So, try engaging students' senses through a *relational memory*. According to Willis (2008), relational memory is the process of connecting new experiences to something we already have in our stored memory. For example, you can connect the feeling of the wind in your face while riding in a car with the windows down to the feeling of the wind blowing in your face while riding a bike.

Strategy Insight

Students are shown a picture and then asked to imagine that they are in the picture. They are asked to describe what they see. When teachers are working with students on this skill, they should keep asking, "What else do you see?" This reminds students to pay attention to detail. Since paying attention is a skill that has to be taught, teachers can work with students by giving them practice that is engaging, particularly if they choose pictures that are colorful, unusual, close up, or intriguing (Jensen 2006). The right brain creates the gist, or context of experiences, and the overall meaning of events (Siegel 2001). As students pay attention to the details, the teacher should be prepared to be amazed at what students can pick out! The teacher can continue the strategy by asking students to consider what they might touch, hear, smell, or taste. If students say "I think it would sound loud" when looking at a picture of a busy city with cars bumper-to-bumper, then the teacher can ask, "What do you see that supports your thinking?" It is beneficial for students to do the thinking and articulate the reasoning behind their thinking. The goal is to increase engagement, improve their attention to detail, tap in to the emotions of what it would be like to be in the picture, and use multiple senses to help remember.

Teacher Notes

◎ At the start of the lesson, use a picture that is engaging and one that students have experience with as you walk through the process.

◎ Understand that modeling is required for students to learn how to identify background knowledge, relate it to what they know, or imagine the experience of what it would be like to be "in" the picture.

Just Say It
Strategy Overview

Working together and hearing thoughts and language are beneficial to all learners, but these things can be especially beneficial to English language learners. *Just Say It* permits students not only to use what they have read, written, or heard but to have a chance to use listening skills for the content, as well. A challenge layer to this strategy is having students hold back on a response for a period of time. This allows the one student to say what he or she needs to say before the partner inflicts his or her opinion or factual information upon him or her. It teaches the skill of patience, listening, and being open to others' thoughts at the same time.

Strategy Insight

Students are to respond to their partners, providing feedback and information on a given topic (e.g., a writing prompt, thoughts, an idea). Have students sit facing their partners (sitting at desks is preferable). Identify Partner *A* as the person closest to the front of the room and Partner *B* as the person closest to the back of room. Have Partner *A* start. Partner *A* shares his or her thinking with Partner *B* as Partner *B* only listens for 30 seconds. After 30 seconds, Partner *B* responds to Partner *A*. They then switch roles—Partner *B* shares while *A* listens. Then, *A* provides insight or feedback. Students should record (during or at the end), what their partners say for further consideration and use that to write about the topic.

Teacher Notes

◎ You may wish to shorten or lengthen the time each partner has, depending upon the topic and age.

◎ Using a timer, a train whistle, or a bell is a great way to help partners know when to switch, since conversations may get lively or partners may tune out other nearby sounds.

How to Use This Book

Lesson Overview

The following lesson components are in each lesson and establish the flow and success of the lessons.

Icons state the brain-powered strategy and one of the four content areas addressed in the book: language arts, mathematics, science, or social studies.

Each lesson revolves around one of the eight **brain-powered strategies** in this book. Be sure to review the description of each strategy found on pages 12–19.

Vocabulary that will be addressed in the lesson is called out in case extra support is needed.

The **procedures** provide step-by-step instructions on how to implement the lessons successfully.

The **standard** indicates the objective for the lesson.

A **materials** list identifies the components of the lesson.

Many lessons contain a **preparation note** that indicates action needed prior to implementing the lessons. Be sure to review these notes to ensure a successful delivery of the lesson.

The **model** section of the lesson provides teachers the opportunity to model what is expected of students and what needs to be accomplished throughout the lesson.

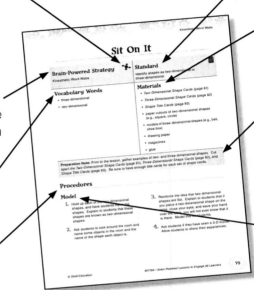

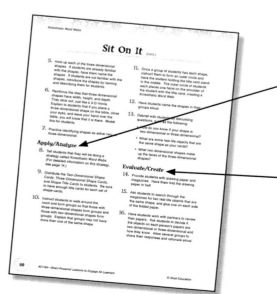

The **apply/analyze** section of the lesson provides students with the opportunity to apply what they are learning as they analyze the content and work toward creating a personal connection.

The **evaluate/create** section of the lesson provides students with the opportunity to think critically about the work of others and then to take ownership of their learning by designing the content in a way that makes sense to them.

How to Use This Book *(cont.)*

Lesson Overview *(cont.)*

Some lessons require **activity cards** to be used. You may wish to laminate the activity cards for added durability. Be sure to read the preparation note in each lesson to prepare the activity cards, when applicable.

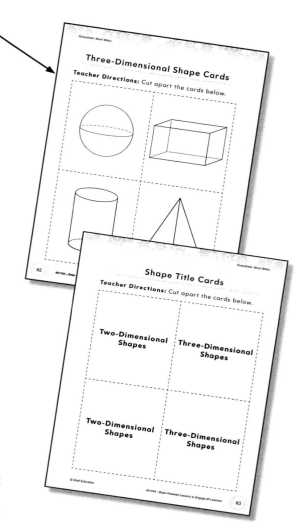

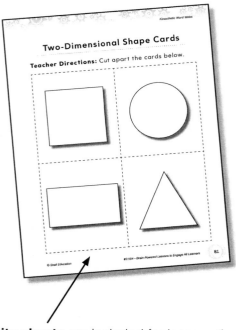

Activity sheets are included for lessons that require them. They are to be used either in groups, individually, or just by the teacher. If students are working in groups, encourage them to create a group name to label the activity sheet.

All of the activity sheets and additional teacher resources can be found on the **Digital Resource CD**.

How to Use This Book *(cont.)*

Implementing Higher-Order Thinking in the Lessons

What Is Higher-Order Thinking?

Higher-order thinking occurs on a different level than memorizing facts or telling something back to someone exactly the way it was told (Thomas and Thorne 2009). As educators, it is important to be aware of the level of thinking that students are asked to do. If teachers record the number of questions they ask students on a recall or restate level as well as how many were asked at a higher level, they may be surprised at the imbalance. How do they expect students to think at a higher level if they are not challenged with higher-order questions and problems? Students should be given questions and assignments that require higher-order thinking.

Higher-order thinking also involves critical thinking. If teachers want students to remember facts and think critically, they need to have them be engaged and working with the content at a higher level so that it creates understanding and depth. In addition, higher-order thinking and critical thinking are imperative to 21st century skills. Employers want workers who can problem-solve and work cooperatively to find multiple solutions. The lessons in this resource gradually place more ownership of the learning process in the hands of students as they simultaneously move through higher-order thinking.

Bloom's Taxonomy and Webb's Depth of Knowledge

Throughout the history of education, structures were created to guide teachers in ways to evoke higher-order thinking. Two of the more popular structures are Bloom's Taxonomy and Webb's Depth of Knowledge (DOK).

Benjamin Bloom developed Bloom's Taxonomy as a way to classify educational learning objectives in a hierarchy. In 2001, Lorin Anderson, a former student of Bloom's, worked with some teachers to revise Bloom's original taxonomy by changing the terminology into verbs and switching the top two levels so that *create* (synthesis) is at the top and *evaluate* (evaluation) is just below (Overbaugh and Schultz n.d.).

Norman Webb created Depth of Knowledge in 1997 in order to assist with aligning the depth and complexity of a standard with its assessment. This structure focuses on how the verb is used in the context of what is asked of the student (Webb 2005). DOK correlates with Backwards Planning (Wiggins and McTighe 2005) in that the standards are addressed first and then an assessment that targets the standards is developed or selected.

How to Use This Book *(cont.)*

It is important that teachers instruct students at cognitive levels that meet their needs while challenging them, as well. Whether students are below level, on level, or above level, teachers should use the tools necessary to help them succeed. Using Webb's DOK gives us the tools to look at the end result and tie complexity to the assessment. Bloom's Taxonomy helps to guide depth of assignments and questions. Where the two meet is with the word complexity. Complexity is rigor. Complexity is the changing of levels within Bloom's, and DOK is the amount of depth of thinking that must occur. We want rigor, and thus, we want complexity in our teachings.

Bloom's Taxonomy	Webb's Depth of Knowledge
Knowledge/Remembering The recall of specifics and universals, involving little more than bringing to mind the appropriate material.	**Recall** The recall of a fact, information, or procedure (e.g., What are three critical-skill cues for the overhand throw?).
Comprehension/Understanding The ability to process knowledge on a low level such that the knowledge can be reproduced or communicated without a verbatim repetition.	**Skill/Concept** The use of information, conceptual knowledge, procedures, two or more steps, etc.
Application/Applying The ability to use information in another familiar situation.	**Strategy Thinking** Requires reasoning, developing a plan, or sequence of steps; has some complexity; more than one possible answer.
Analysis/Analyzing The ability to break information into parts to explore understandings and relationships.	**Extended Thinking** Requires an investigation as well as time to think and process multiple conditions of the problem or task.
Synthesis and Evaluation/Evaluating and Creating Putting together elements and parts to form a whole and then making value judgements about the method.	

Adapted from Wyoming School Health and Physical Education (2001)

Correlation to the Standards

Shell Education is committed to producing educational materials that are research and standards based. In this effort, we have correlated all of our products to the academic standards of all 50 states, the District of Columbia, the Department of Defense Dependents Schools, and all Canadian provinces.

How to Find Standards Correlations

To print a customized correlation report of this product for your state, visit our website at http://www.shelleducation.com and follow the on-screen directions. If you require assistance in printing correlation reports, please contact our Customer Service department at 1-877-777-3450.

Purpose and Intent of Standards

Legislation mandates that all states adopt academic standards that identify the skills students will learn in kindergarten through grade twelve. Many states also have standards for Pre–K. This same legislation sets requirements to ensure the standards are detailed and comprehensive.

Standards are designed to focus instruction and guide adoption of curricula. Standards are statements that describe the criteria necessary for students to meet specific academic goals. They define the knowledge, skills, and content students should acquire at each level. Standards are also used to develop standardized tests to evaluate students' academic progress. Teachers are required to demonstrate how their lessons meet state standards. State standards are used in the development of all of our products, so educators can be assured they meet the academic requirements of each state.

Common Core State Standards

Many lessons in this book are aligned to the Common Core State Standards (CCSS). The standards support the objectives presented throughout the lessons and are provided on the Digital Resource CD (filename: standards.pdf).

TESOL and WIDA Standards

The lessons in this book promote English language development for English language learners. The standards listed on the Digital Resource CD (filename: standards.pdf) support the language objectives presented throughout the lessons.

Standards Chart

Common Core State Standard	Lesson(s)
Reading: Foundational Skills K.2.a—Recognize and produce rhyming words	Rhyme Time p. 29
Reading: Informational Text K.5—Identify the front cover, back cover, and title page of a book	Parts of a Book p. 73
Reading: Informational Text K.6—Name the author and illustrator of a text and define the role of each in presenting the ideas or information in a text	Parts of a Book p. 73
Reading: Literature K.2—With prompting and support, retell familiar stories, including key details	Story Retell p. 126
Reading: Literature K.5—Recognize common types of texts	Text Types p. 96
Reading: Literature K.9—With prompting and support, compare and contrast the adventures and experiences of characters in familiar stories	Compare and Contrast p. 61
Writing K.1—Use a combination of drawings, dictating, and writing to compose opinion pieces in which they tell a reader the topic or name of the book they are writing about and state an opinion or preference about the topic or book	Favorite Character p. 132
Writing K.2—Use a combination of drawing, dictating, and writing to compose informative/explanatory texts in which they name what they are writing about and supply some information about the topic	Get Detailed p. 102
Writing K.5—With guidance and support from adults, respond to questions and suggestions from peers and add details to strengthen writing as needed	Add Details p. 143; So What Do You Think? p. 152
Math K.CC.1—Count to 100 by ones and by tens	Counting p. 128
Math K.CC.3—Write numbers from 0 to 20. Represent a number of objects with a written numeral 0–20	Count It p. 40
Math K.OA.3—Decompose numbers less than or equal to 10 into pairs in more than one way, e.g., by using objects or drawings, and record each decomposition by drawing or equation	Give Me Ten p. 136

Standards Chart *(cont.)*

Common Core State Standard	Lesson(s)
Math K.MD.2—Directly compare two objects with a measurable attribute in common, to see which object has "more of"/"less of" the attribute, and describe the difference	Describe It p. 154
Math K.G.3—Identify shapes as two-dimensional or three-dimensional	Sit On It p. 79
Math K.G.4—Analyze and compare two- and three-dimensional shapes, in different sizes and orientations, using informal language to describe their similarities, differences, parts, and other attributes	The Shape of Things p. 68

McREL Standard	Lesson(s)
Science 1.1—Knows vocabulary for different types of weather	Wonderful Weather p. 112
Science 10.3—Knows that the position of an object can be described by locating it relative to another object or the background	Where Is It? p. 139
Science 8.2—Sorts objects based on observable properties	Too Hot, Too Cold p. 64
Science 10.4—Knows that the position and motion of an object can be changed by pushing or pulling	Push and Pull p. 84
Science 12.1—Uses the senses to make observations about living things, nonliving objects, and events	Sensational Senses p. 54
History 1.2—Understands family life today and how it compares with family life in the recent past and family life long ago	What Was It Like? p. 148
History 2.1—Understands changes in community over time	Then and Now p. 90
History 4.4—Knows how different groups of people in the community have taken responsibility for the common good (e.g., the police department, the fire department, senior citizen home, soup kitchen)	Community Workers p. 118

Standards Chart *(cont.)*

McREL Standard	Lesson(s)
Geography 1.0—Understands characteristics and uses of maps, globes, and other geographic tools and technologies	Land and Water p. 141
Geography 4.1—Knows the physical and human characteristics of the local community	It's In the Community p. 156

TESOL and WIDA Standard	Lesson(s)
English language learners **communicate** for **social, intercultural,** and **instructional** purposes within the school setting	All Lessons
English language learners **communicate** information, ideas, and concepts necessary for academic success in the area of **language arts**	All Lessons

Content Area Correlations Chart

Content Area	Lessons
Reading	Rhyme Time p. 29; Compare and Contrast p. 61; Parts of a Book p. 73; Text Types p. 96; Story Retell p. 126
Writing	Get Detailed p. 102; Favorite Character p. 132; Add Details p. 143; So, What Do You Think? p. 152
Math	Count It p. 40; The Shape of Things p. 68; Sit On It p. 79; Counting p. 128; Give Me Ten p. 136; Describe It p. 154
Social Studies	Then and Now p. 90; Community Workers p. 118; Land and Water p. 141; What Was It Like? p. 148; It's In the Community p. 156
Science	Sensational Senses p. 54; Too Hot, Too Cold p. 64; Push and Pull p. 84; Wonderful Weather p. 112; Where Is It? p. 139

Rhyme Time

Brain-Powered Strategy	**Standard**
Sort It	Recognize and produce rhyming words

Vocabulary Words

- rhyme
- sounds

Materials

- *Rhyme Time Cards* (pages 31–39)
- rhyming book or song (e.g., *The Cat in the Hat* by Dr. Seuss)
- chart paper
- music (*optional*)

Preparation Note: Prior to the lesson, photocopy and cut apart the *Rhyme Time Cards* (pages 31–39). Have enough available so each student can have a card and so that there is a corresponding rhyme for each picture used.

Procedures

Model

1. Read the selected rhyming book or song to students. As you are reading, pause just before you read or sing a word that rhymes, and have students help supply the missing word.

2. You may wish to record a list of the rhyming words students heard.

3. Review with students that rhyming words are words that end with the same sounds. Say several pairs of rhyming words from the book or song, emphasizing the ending sounds.

4. Draw quick pictures of a bun, a star, and a sun on the board or on a sheet of chart paper.

5. Tell students that two of the pictures rhyme or sound the same. Say the words *bun* and *star*. Emphasize the ending sound of each word. Tell students that you hear *-un* at the end of *bun* and *-ar* at the end of *star*.

6. Say the words *bun* and *sun*. Emphasize the ending sound of each word. Tell students you hear *-un* at the end of *bun* and *sun*, so these words rhyme. Circle the bun and sun pictures to show they rhyme.

7. Repeat Steps 5–6, as needed, using other rhyming words and non-rhyming words.

Rhyme Time *(cont.)*

Apply/Analyze

8. Distribute the *Rhyme Time Cards*, one to each student. Have students name the pictures shown on their cards.

9. Tell students that they will be doing a strategy called *Sort It*. (For detailed information on this strategy, see page 12.) Explain to students that they should find another student who has a picture that rhymes with the picture on their card.

10. Play music as students mingle around the room. Once students have sorted themselves, have pairs of students say the names of the pictures on their cards aloud so the whole class can hear the rhymes.

11. Redistribute the cards and have students play again.

Evaluate/Create

12. Have pairs of students keep the cards they use for the last round played.

13. Have students work together to think of one more word that rhymes and one word that does not rhyme with the pair of words they had.

14. Ask students to be ready to share aloud the three words that rhyme and the one word that does not rhyme and be able to explain why it does not rhyme.

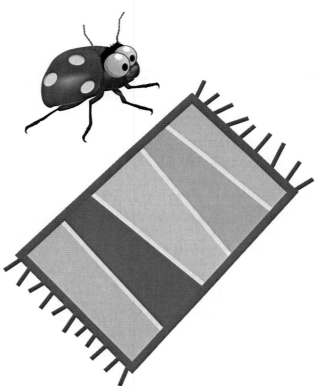

Rhyme Time Cards

Teacher Directions: Cut apart the cards below.

Rhyme Time Cards *(cont.)*

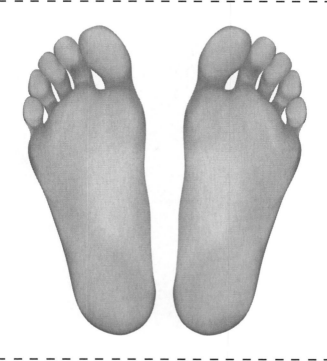

Rhyme Time Cards *(cont.)*

Rhyme Time Cards *(cont.)*

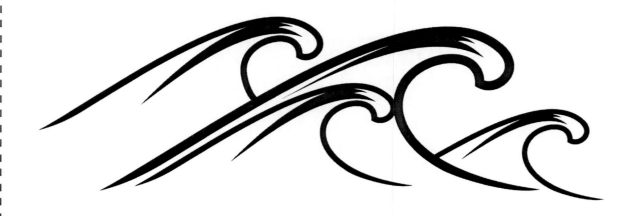

Rhyme Time Cards *(cont.)*

Rhyme Time Cards *(cont.)*

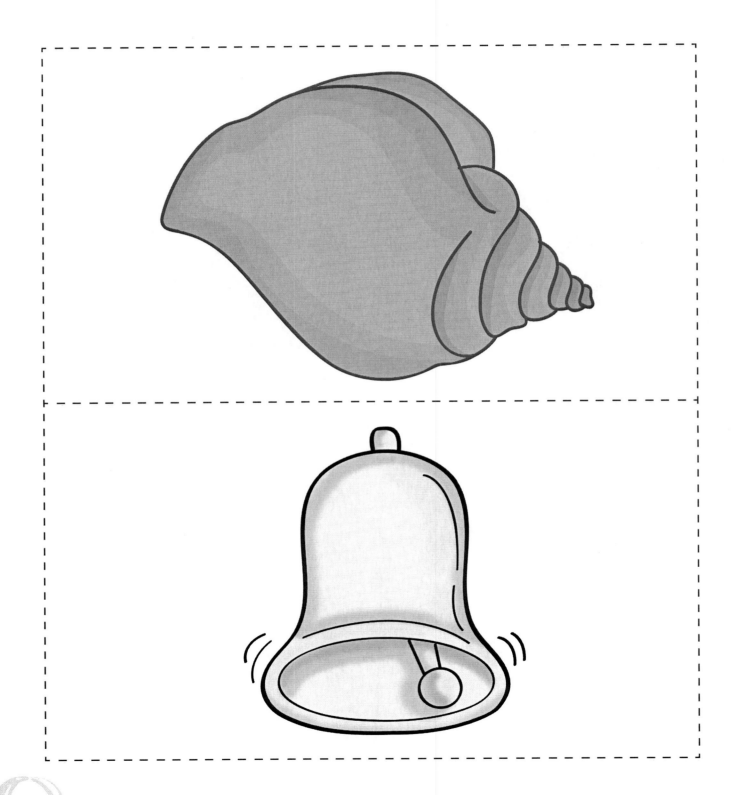

Rhyme Time Cards *(cont.)*

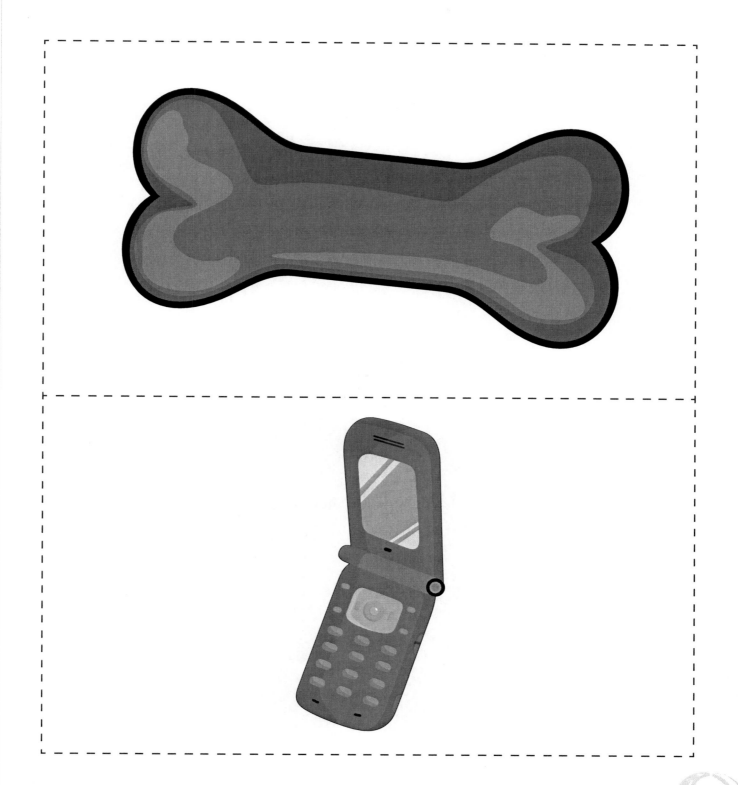

Rhyme Time Cards (cont.)

Rhyme Time Cards *(cont.)*

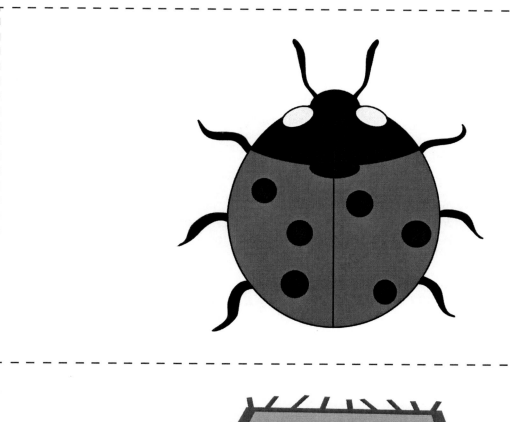

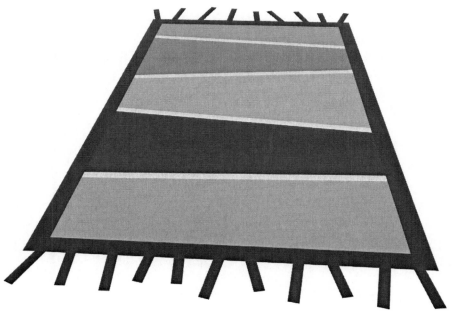

Count It

Brain-Powered Strategy	**Standard**
Sort It	Write numbers from 0 to 20. Represent a number of objects with a written numeral 0–20.

Vocabulary Words

- count
- number
- numeral

Materials

- *Count It Cards* (pages 42–53)
- chart paper
- drawing paper
- crayons or markers
- music (*optional*)

Preparation Note: Prior to the lesson, photocopy and cut apart the *Count It Cards* (pages 42–53). Have enough available so that each student can have a card and so that each numeral card has a corresponding number card. You may have more than one copy of the same numeral/number.

Procedures

Model

1. Display the numerals from the *Count It Cards*. Have students count from 0–20 aloud together.

2. Draw five stars on the board or on a sheet of chart paper. Ask students to count the stars aloud with you as you point to each one. Tell students that the number of stars that are on the board is five.

3. Write the numeral five on the board next to the stars. Explain that the numeral five is a symbol that shows how many stars there are.

4. Repeat Steps 2–3 as needed.

Count It *(cont.)*

Apply/Analyze

5. Distribute the *Count It Cards*, one to each student. Have students identify the numerals or count the objects on their cards.

6. Tell students that they will be doing a strategy called *Sort It*. (For detailed information on this strategy, see page 12.) Explain to students that they should match the number of objects to the numerals shown.

7. Play music as students mingle around the room. Once students have sorted themselves, have them share with each other why they belong together.

8. Collect, shuffle, and redistribute the cards. Have students play again.

Evaluate/Create

9. Provide students with drawing paper. Model for students how to fold the paper in half.

10. Ask students to choose a numeral from 0–20 to write on the left side of their paper. Have students choose a simple object, such as a smiley face or flower, and draw the same number of objects on the right side of the paper.

11. Divide students into groups of two to three. Have students compare their drawings. Which person in the group has the largest numeral? How do they know? Which person in the group has the smallest numeral? How do they know?

Count It Cards

Teacher Directions: Cut apart the cards below.

1

Count It Cards *(cont.)*

2

Count It Cards *(cont.)*

3

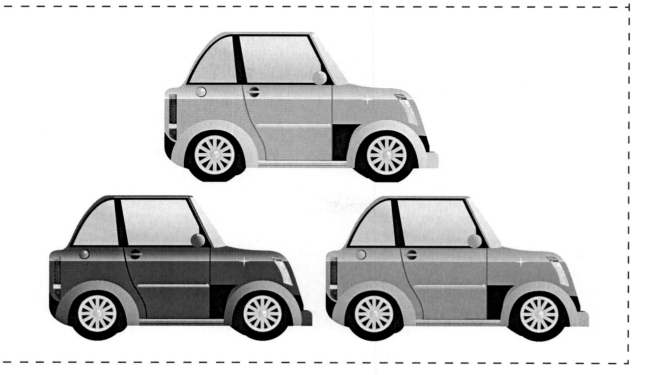

Count It Cards *(cont.)*

4

Count It Cards *(cont.)*

5

Count It Cards (cont.)

6

Count It Cards *(cont.)*

7

Count It Cards *(cont.)*

8

Count It Cards (cont.)

9

Count It Cards *(cont.)*

10

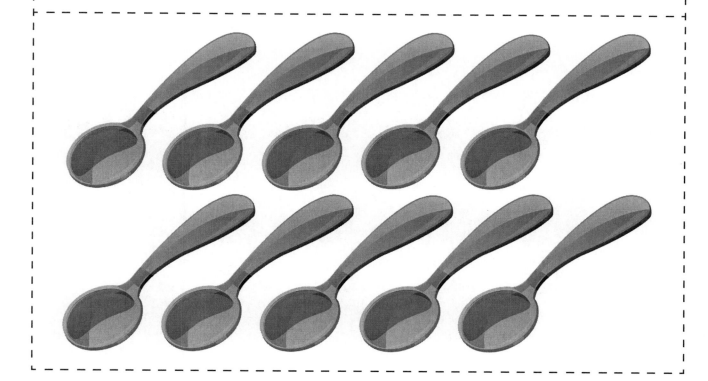

Count It Cards *(cont.)*

11

Count It Cards *(cont.)*

12

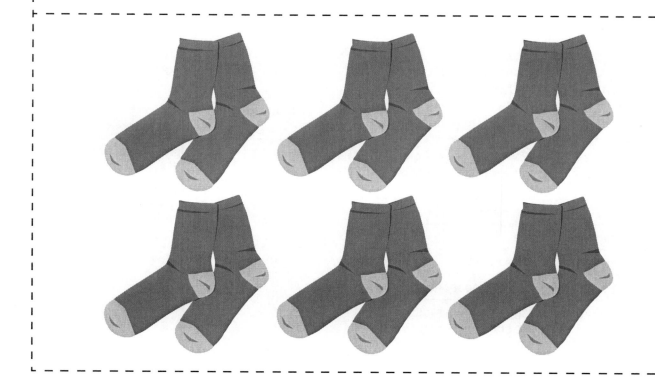

Sensational Senses

Brain-Powered Strategy	**Standard**
Sort It	Uses the senses to make observations about living things, nonliving objects, and events

Vocabulary Words

- hear
- senses
- sight
- smell
- taste
- touch

Materials

- *Sensational Senses Cards* (pages 56–60)
- chart paper
- several photographs or pictures of objects
- sticky notes
- music (*optional*)

Preparation Note: Prior to the lesson, photocopy and cut out the *Sensational Senses Cards* (pages 56–60). Have enough available so each student can have a card. You may have more than one copy of the same word or picture.

Procedures

Model

1. Explain to students that there are five parts of our body that help us learn about the world. List the five senses on the board or on a sheet of chart paper.

2. Show students a quick way to remember the five senses with their hands. Have students use the following fingers of one hand to touch the corresponding body part:

thumb	ear, hear
index finger	eye, see
middle finger	nose, smell
ring finger	mouth/tongue, taste
little finger	wiggle in the air just below the chin to indicate touch

3. Provide students examples of each of the senses being used. Discuss each sense as you provide the example. For example:

hearing	cup your hand up to your ear
seeing	stare at an object in the room
smelling	sniff the air
tasting	pretend to lick an ice cream cone
touching	stroke your hair or arm

Sensational Senses *(cont.)*

4. Model examples of the senses in use. For example, when you see a delicious apple, you are using your eyes and your sense of seeing and when a skunk sprays a stinky scent, you use your nose to smell it. Continue providing examples, as needed.

Apply/Analyze

5. Distribute the *Sensational Senses Cards*, one to each student. Have students name the pictures shown on their cards.

6. Tell students that they will be doing a strategy called *Sort It*. (For detailed information on this strategy, see page 12.) Explain to students that they should match sense words to the pictures of the corresponding body parts.

7. Play music as students mingle around the room. Once students have sorted themselves, have pairs of students use the following sentence frame to share about their senses and the corresponding body parts: *We use our _____ to _____.* (e.g., *We use our <u>nose</u> to <u>smell</u>.*)

8. Redistribute the cards and have students play again.

Evaluate/Create

9. Divide students into groups of three to four for discussion.

10. Display a picture or photograph of an object. Ask each group to determine which sense would be best to use to describe the object. Have them brainstorm their ideas.

11. Gather the class back together, and allow each group to share what they discussed. After hearing all of the groups' presentations, provide each student with a sticky note, and have them write the sense that they now feel would be the best to use to describe the objects. Tally and report the results to the class.

12. Repeat Steps 10–11 with other pictures or photographs.

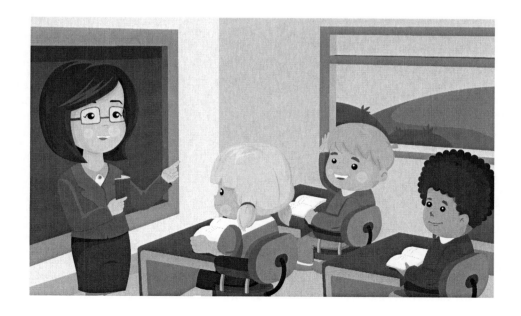

Sensational Senses Cards

Teacher Directions: Cut apart the cards below.

hear

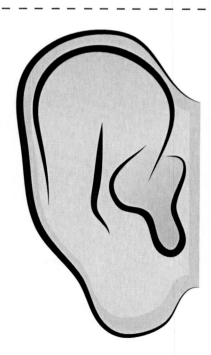

Sensational Senses Cards *(cont.)*

see

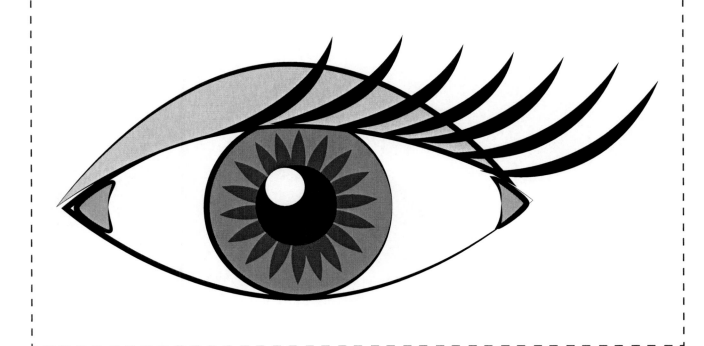

Sensational Senses Cards *(cont.)*

smell

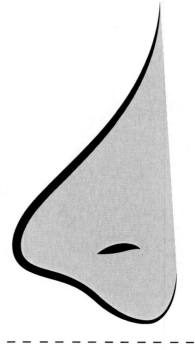

#51184—*Brain-Powered Lessons to Engage All Learners* © *Shell Education*

Sensational Senses Cards *(cont.)*

taste

Sensational Senses Cards *(cont.)*

touch

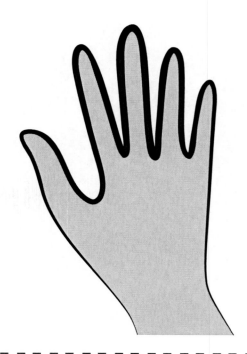

Compare and Contrast

Brain-Powered Strategy	**Standard**
It Takes Two	With prompting and support, compare and contrast the adventures and experiences of characters in familiar stories

Vocabulary Words

- alike
- compare
- contrast
- different

Materials

- *Alike and Different Books* (page 63)
- chart
- an apple and an orange (or two other objects that are tangible and easy to compare and contrast)
- two books that can be used for compare and contrast (e.g., *Goldilocks and the Three Bears* and *Somebody and the Three Blairs*)
- sticky notes

Preparation Note: Prior to the lesson, create a two-column chart on a sheet of chart paper. Label one of the columns *Alike* and the other column *Different*.

Procedures

Model

1. Display the apple and ask students to describe it. Put the apple away, and repeat with the orange.

2. Display the apple and the orange side-by-side. Explain to students that one way to talk about the apple and the orange is to compare and contrast them. Tell students that *compare* means to tell what is the same and *contrast* means to tell what is different.

3. Have students compare and contrast the apple and the orange. You may wish to provide the following sentence frames to guide the discussion:

   - *The apple and the orange are both _____.*
   - *The apple is _____ and the orange is _____.*

4. Read aloud the first book that will be used for compare and contrast. Thoroughly discuss the characters and plot of the book.

Compare and Contrast *(cont.)*

5. Read aloud the second book either on the same day or a separate day. Thoroughly discuss the characters and plot of the book.

6. Explain to students that although the class has thoroughly discussed each book, another way to discuss books that are similar is to compare and contrast them.

7. Remind students that *compare* means to tell what is the same and *contrast* means to tell what is different.

Apply/Analyze

8. Display the two-column chart, and distribute sticky notes to students.

9. Tell students that they will be doing a strategy called *It Takes Two*. (For detailed information on this strategy, see page 13.)

10. Have each student draw a picture of something from the two stories that is alike or something that is different on his or her sticky note.

11. Invite students to come to the chart and place their sticky notes in the appropriate column. Have students share what their picture is and why they placed it under alike/different. Provide the following sentence frame, if needed, to assist students in articulating their thoughts:

- *Both books have _____.*

- *_____ and _____ are different in the books.*

Sentence frames can be made more complex as needed based on the group of students or time of year. For example:

- *In (name of the book) and (name of the other book) _____ is the same.*

- *In (name of the book) _____ is different than in (name of the other book).*

Evaluate/Create

12. Distribute the *Alike and Different Books* activity sheet (page 63) to students. Ask students to draw and write about one way the books are alike and one way the books are different. Provide time for students to work and be ready to share evidence from the books (with teacher support). Allow several students to share their ideas.

13. Ask students to think of one experience they have had in their own lives that is the same as a character in one of the two books the class read. If students cannot think of an experience that is the same, have them think of an experience from one of the books that they have never had and explain why they would not have been able to have that particular experience. For example, students could explain that they have never been to the setting of the book or they do not have a younger brother or sister.

14. Ask volunteers or select several students to share their responses with the whole class.

Name: _____ **Date:** _____

Alike and Different Books

Directions: Draw and write one way the books are alike and one way they are different.

Alike	Different

Too Hot, Too Cold

Brain-Powered Strategy	Standard
It Takes Two	Sorts objects based on observable properties
Vocabulary Words	**Materials**
• cold • hot • property • temperature	• *Temperature Pictures* (page 66) • *Temperature Sort Mat* (page 67) • *Goldilocks and the Three Bears* (any version) • chart paper • ice cubes • cup of warm water • sticky notes • glue

Preparation Note: Prior to the lesson, create a two-column chart on a sheet of chart paper. Label one of the columns *Hot* and the other column *Cold*.

Procedures

Model

1. Tell students that *temperature* tells how hot or cold something is.

2. Read aloud *Goldilocks and the Three Bears* to students. Before you read, ask students to listen for temperature words such as *cold* and *hot* in the story. After you read, discuss the words that told about the temperature of the porridge.

3. Provide a few ice cubes to students so they can pass them around. Ask students to describe how the ice cubes feel (cold). Once they are done describing the ice cubes, have students dispose of them in the classroom sink, or have student volunteers place them outside the classroom.

4. Hold the cup of lukewarm water, and ask students to come feel the water. Cautiously, have one student at a time place his or her index finger inside the cup to feel the water. Ask students to describe how the water feels (warm).

5. Tell students *hot* and *cold* are words that tell about the temperature of an object. Explain that these are properties of the object.

Too Hot, Too Cold *(cont.)*

Apply/Analyze

6. Display the previously prepared two-column chart, and distribute sticky notes to students.

7. Tell students that they will be doing a strategy called *It Takes Two*. (For detailed information on this strategy, see page 13.)

8. Have each student draw a picture of an object that is either hot or cold on his or her sticky note.

9. Invite students to come to the chart and place their sticky notes in the correct column. Have students share what their object is and why they placed it under hot/cold. Provide the following sentence frame, if needed, to assist students in articulating their thoughts: (Name of object) is hot/cold.

Evaluate/Create

10. Distribute the *Temperature Pictures* activity sheet (page 66) and the *Temperature Sort Mat* activity sheet (page 67). Ask students to cut apart the picture cards.

11. Have students sort the picture cards under the appropriate column by the object's temperature. Rotate around the room as students complete the task to visually evaluate students' understanding of the concept.

12. Have students share their responses with partners, and correct any answers if needed. Once partners agree that their sorting is correct, have students determine which object is the hottest and which one is the coldest, and why or how they know.

13. Divide students into small groups, and allow each group to share their ideas.

Temperature Pictures

Directions: Cut apart the picture cards below.

Name: _____   Date: _____

Temperature Sort Mat

Directions: Sort the picture cards on the mat below.

Hot	Cold

The Shape of Things

Brain-Powered Strategy	**Standard**
It Takes Two	Analyze and compare two- and three-dimensional shapes, in different sizes and orientations, using informal language to describe their similarities, differences, parts, and other attributes

Vocabulary Words	**Materials**
• sides • two-dimensional • vertex	• *Shapes!* (pages 70–72) • chart paper • shape manipulatives (*optional*) • sticky notes • drawing paper

Preparation Note: Prior to the lesson, create a two-column chart on a sheet of chart paper. Label one of the columns *More than Four Sides* and the other column *Less than Four Sides*. Additionally, cut apart the *Shapes!* cards (page 70–72).

Procedures

Model

1. Draw a triangle on the board or on a sheet of chart paper. If available, distribute shape manipulatives so students can actually touch the shapes. Name the shape for students.

2. Continue with other shapes such as a square, a rectangle, a circle, and a trapezoid. Display the shapes from the *Shapes!* cards, so students can reference them throughout the lesson.

3. Explain to students that the straight lines on the triangle are called *sides*. Trace the sides with your finger and have students count the number of sides aloud with you.

4. Tell students that the point where the two sides come together is called a *vertex*. Circle all the vertices on the triangle as students count the number of vertices aloud with you.

5. Repeat Steps 3–4 for the other shapes.

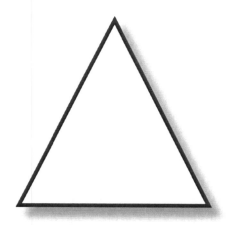

The Shape of Things *(cont.)*

Apply/Analyze

6. Display the two-column chart, and distribute sticky notes to students.

7. Tell students that they will be doing a strategy called *It Takes Two*. (For detailed information on this strategy, see page 13.)

8. Ask students to choose one shape from those on display and draw it on their sticky notes. Give students time to think about in which columns their shapes will be placed. Provide the following sentence frames for students to help them articulate their findings:

- A *(name of shape)* has *(number of sides)*.

- *(Number of sides)* is *(less than/equal to)* 4.

9. Have students bring their sticky notes to the front of the classroom, and place them on the chart in the correct column. As students place their sticky notes on the chart, have them share the completed sentence frame aloud.

10. Continue with other criteria for shapes as needed, such as the number of vertices or equal sides/not equal sides.

Evaluate/Create

11. Provide additional sticky notes (or drawing paper) to students. Have them each draw a different shape than the previously drawn shape.

12. Have students work with partners to identify any similarities and differences between the two shapes they have. Allow partners to share their findings aloud.

13. Rotate students to new partners and repeat Step 12.

Shapes!

Teacher Directions: Cut apart the shapes below.

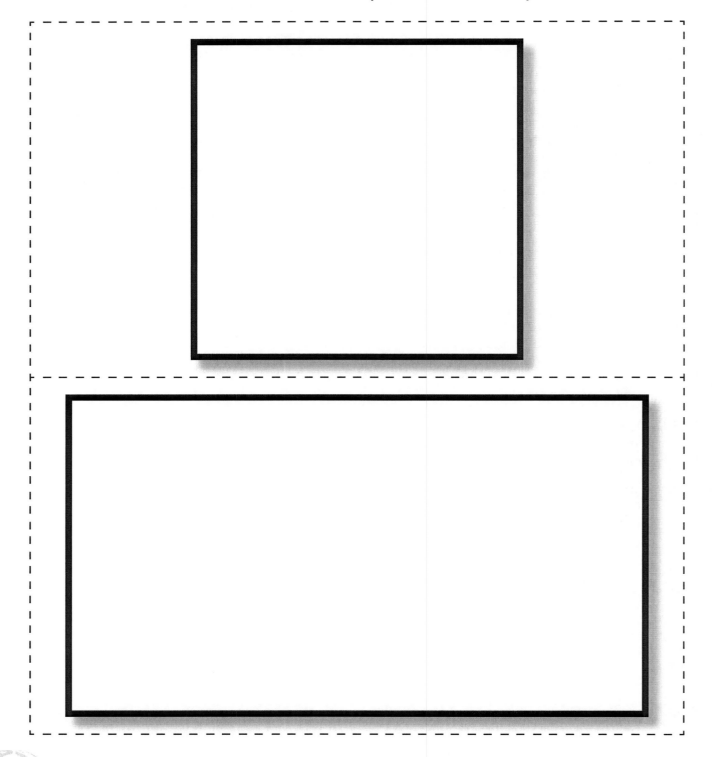

Shapes! *(cont.)*

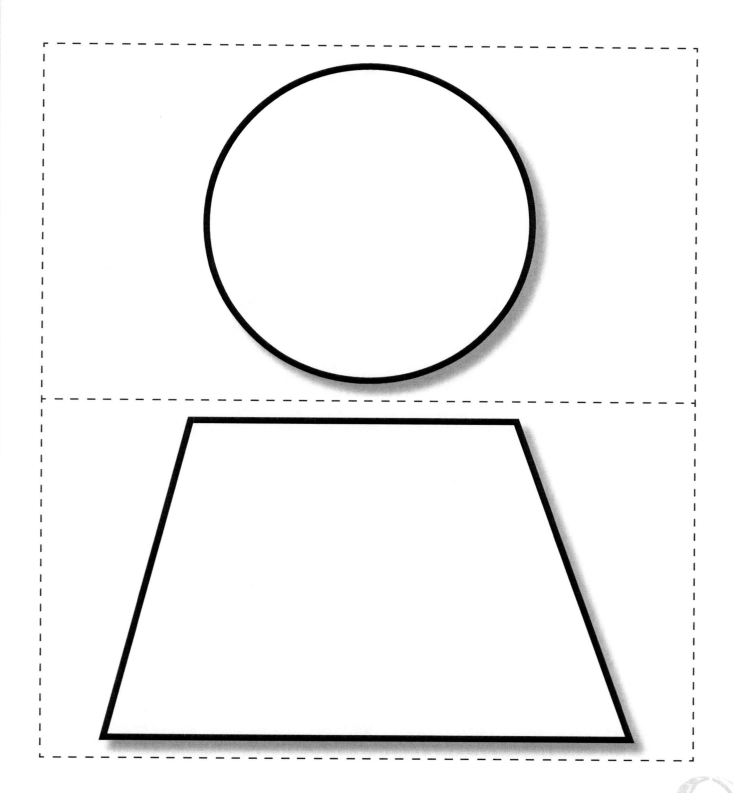

Shapes! *(cont.)*

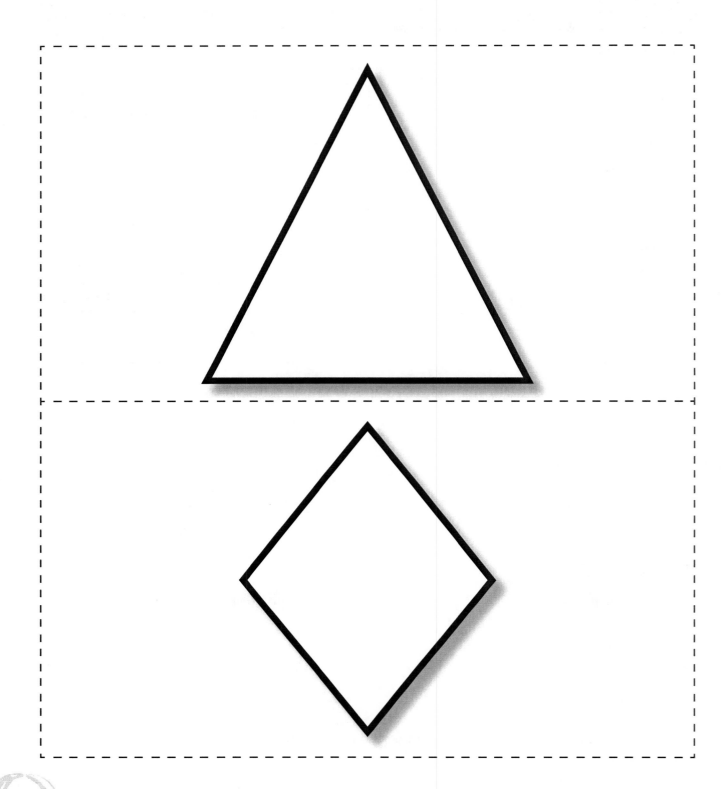

Parts of a Book

Brain-Powered Strategy

Kinesthetic Word Webs

Standards

Identify the front cover, back cover, and title page of a book

Name the author and illustrator of a text and define the role of each in presenting the ideas or information in a text

Vocabulary Words

- author
- back cover
- front cover
- illustrator

Materials

- *Book Cards* (pages 75–78)
- index cards
- books (any titles)

Preparation Note: Prior to the lesson, cut apart the *Book Cards* (pages 75–78). Also, write each of the following on index cards: *Dinosaur Days*, *Inventions*, *Bugs*, *Antarctica*.

Procedures

Model

1. Sing the song and do the hand motions for *Head and Shoulders, Knees, and Toes*.

2. Discuss what head, shoulders, knees, and toes are parts of (the body). Have students name other parts of their bodies.

3. Explain to students that just like their bodies, books have different parts to them, too.

4. Hold up a book to use as a model. It is helpful to use a book students are very familiar with. Point out for students the various parts of the book and explain the functions of each part:

   - front cover
   - back cover
   - author
   - illustrator/photographer

5. Provide students with books. Students can work alone or with partners. Call out various parts of a book and have students locate the parts on their books. Monitor students as they work to find the book parts.

Parts of a Book *(cont.)*

Apply/Analyze

6. Tell students that they will be doing a strategy called *Kinesthetic Word Webs*. (For detailed information on this strategy, see page 14.)

7. Distribute the previously prepared index cards and the *Book Cards* to students. Be sure to have enough index cards with titles for each set of book cards.

8. Instruct students to walk around the room and form groups so that the parts of the same book are together.

9. Once a group of students has each part of a book, instruct them to form an outer circle and have the student holding the index card with the title stand in the middle. The outer circle of students each place one hand on the shoulder of the student with the title card creating, a *Kinesthetic Word Web*.

10. Have the student in the middle read the title of the book. Have each student in the web tell what part of the book he or she is holding.

11. Debrief with students by discussing questions, such as the following:

- How did you know which book your card belonged to?

- What were some clues that they belonged together in the same group?

Evaluate/Create

12. Divide students into pairs. Provide each pair of students with two books. Have students compare the covers of the two books to identify the placements of the titles, pictures, authors' names, and illustrators' names. Ask students to discuss with their partners why each element of a cover was placed where it was. For example, students may determine that the title was placed in a certain place because of how large the illustration is.

13. Ask students to leave the two books on their desks. Allow students to rotate around the room with their partners to view other pairs of books. Have them discuss the same elements as in Step 12.

14. Have students return to their original desks. Allow several students to describe what was discussed with their partners.

Book Cards

Teacher Directions: Cut apart the cards below.

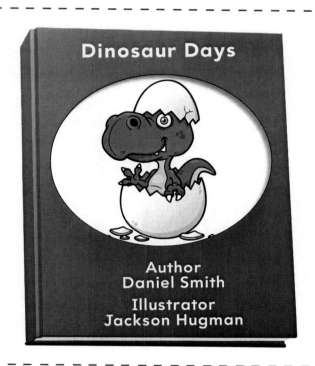

Written by Daniel Smith

Illustrated by Jackson Hugman

Book Cards *(cont.)*

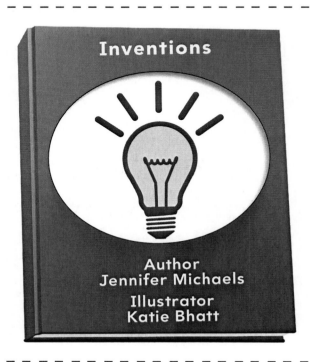

Written by Jennifer Michaels

Illustrated by Katie Bhatt

Book Cards *(cont.)*

Written by John Wendle

Illustrated by Louis Garcia

Book Cards *(cont.)*

Written by Ammie Thatch

Illustrated by Charlotte Pinkman

#51184—Brain-Powered Lessons to Engage All Learners

Sit On It

Brain-Powered Strategy	Standard
Kinesthetic Word Webs	Identify shapes as two-dimensional or three-dimensional

Vocabulary Words

- three-dimensional
- two-dimensional

Materials

- *Two-Dimensional Shape Cards* (page 81)
- *Three-Dimensional Shape Cards* (page 82)
- *Shape Title Cards* (page 83)
- paper cutouts of two-dimensional shapes (e.g., square, circle)
- models of three-dimensional shapes (e.g., ball, shoe box)
- drawing paper
- magazines
- glue

Preparation Note: Prior to the lesson, gather examples of two- and three-dimensional shapes. Cut apart the *Two-Dimensional Shape Cards* (page 81), *Three-Dimensional Shape Cards* (page 82), and *Shape Title Cards* (page 83). Be sure to have enough title cards for each set of shape cards.

Procedures

Model

1. Hold up each of the two-dimensional shapes, and have students name the shapes. Explain to students that these shapes are known as *two-dimensional shapes*.

2. Ask students to look around the room and name some objects in the room and the name of the shape each object is.

3. Reinforce the idea that two-dimensional shapes are flat. Explain to students that if you place a two-dimensional shape on the table, close your eyes, and wave your hand over the table, you will not even know that it is there. Model this for students.

4. Ask students if they have seen a 3-D movie. Allow students to share their experiences.

Sit On It *(cont.)*

5. Hold up each of the three-dimensional shapes. If students are already familiar with the shapes, have them name the shapes. If students are not familiar with the shapes, introduce the shapes by naming and describing them for students.

6. Reinforce the idea that three-dimensional shapes have width, height, and depth. They stick out, just like a 3-D movie. Explain to students that if you place a three-dimensional shape on the table, close your eyes, and wave your hand over the table, you will know that it is there. Model this for students.

7. Practice identifying shapes as either two- or three-dimensional.

Apply/Analyze

8. Tell students that they will be doing a strategy called *Kinesthetic Word Webs*. (For detailed information on this strategy, see page 14.)

9. Distribute the *Two-Dimensional Shape Cards*, *Three-Dimensional Shape Cards*, and *Shape Title Cards* to students. Be sure to have enough title cards for each set of shape cards.

10. Instruct students to walk around the room and form groups so that those with three-dimensional shapes form groups and those with two-dimensional shapes form groups. Explain that groups may not have more than one of the same shape.

11. Once a group of students has each shape, instruct them to form an outer circle and have the student holding the title card stand in the middle. The outer circle of students each places one hand on the shoulder of the student with the title card, creating a *Kinesthetic Word Web*.

12. Have students name the shapes in their groups aloud.

13. Debrief with students by discussing questions, such as the following:

- How do you know if your shape is two-dimensional or three-dimensional?

- What are some real-life objects that are the same shape as your cards?

- What two-dimensional shapes make up the faces of the three-dimensional shapes?

Evaluate/Create

14. Provide students with drawing paper and magazines. Have them fold the drawing paper in half.

15. Ask students to search through the magazines for two real-life objects that are the same shape, and glue one on each side of the folded paper.

16. Have students work with partners to review their papers. Ask students to decide if the objects on each person's papers are two-dimensional or three-dimensional and how they know. Allow several groups to share their responses and rationale aloud.

Two-Dimensional Shape Cards

Teacher Directions: Cut apart the cards below.

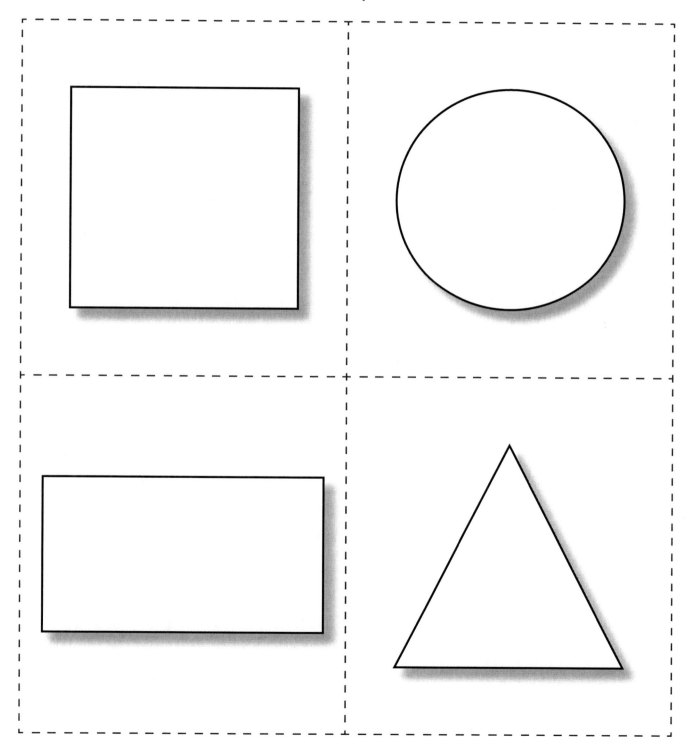

Three-Dimensional Shape Cards

Teacher Directions: Cut apart the cards below.

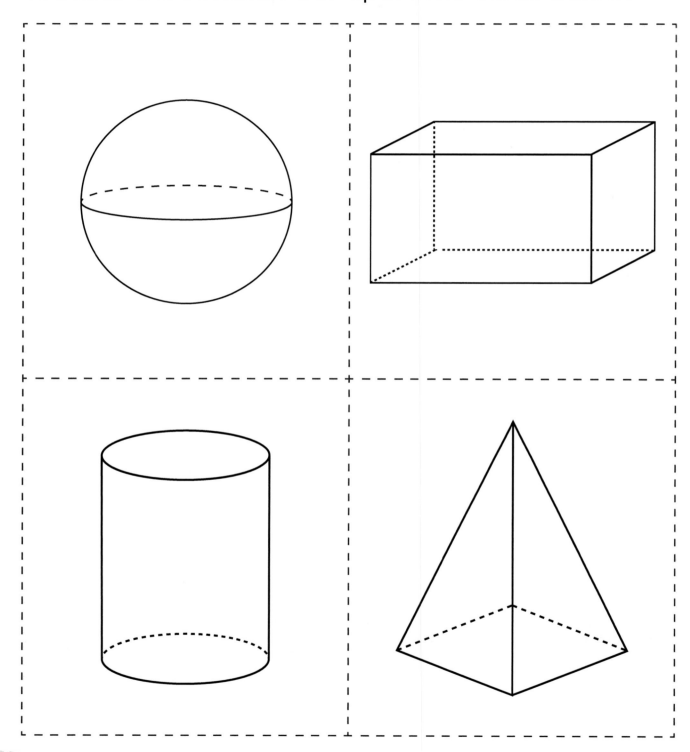

Shape Title Cards

Teacher Directions: Cut apart the cards below.

Two-Dimensional Shapes

Three-Dimensional Shapes

Two-Dimensional Shapes

Three-Dimensional Shapes

Push and Pull

Brain-Powered Strategy	Standard
Kinesthetic Word Webs	Knows that the position and motion of an object can be changed by pushing or pulling

Vocabulary Words

- motion
- position
- pull
- push

Materials

- *Push and Pull Title Cards* (page 86)
- *Push and Pull Picture Cards* (pages 87–89)
- drawing paper
- dominoes

Preparation Note: Prior to the lesson, cut apart the *Push and Pull Title Cards* (page 86) and the *Push and Pull Picture Cards* (pages 87–89). Have enough available so each student can have one card. You may have more than one copy of the same picture if needed.

Procedures

Model

1. Walk over to a drawer or file cabinet in the classroom. Model pulling the drawer open. Discuss what happens to your body as you pull. Discuss what happens to the drawer as you pull as well.

2. Push the drawer shut and again discuss what happens to your body and the drawer.

3. Have students stand behind their chairs. Have students model pushing their chairs back to their desks.

4. Ask them to model pulling the chair away from their desks. Discuss the difference between the two motions.

5. Distribute drawing paper to students. Have them write the capital letter *M* on their papers. Ask them to pay attention to when they are pushing and pulling on the pencil. Have students write more *M*s as needed. Discuss the push and pull needed to write the letter.

6. Ask students to look around the room and identify other things that can be pushed or pulled.

Push and Pull *(cont.)*

Apply/Analyze

7. Tell students that they will be doing a strategy called *Kinesthetic Word Webs*. (For detailed information on this strategy, see page 14.)

8. Provide students with the *Push and Pull Title Cards* and the *Push and Pull Picture Cards*.

9. Instruct students to walk around the room and form groups so that the *Push and Pull Title Cards* and the *Push and Pull Picture Cards* match accordingly. Explain that groups may not have more than one of the same *Push and Pull Title Cards*.

10. Once a group has formed, instruct students to form an outer circle and have the student holding the title card stand in the middle. The outer circle of students each places one hand on the shoulder of the student with the title card, creating a *Kinesthetic Word Web*.

11. Have students name the cards in their groups aloud.

12. Debrief with students by discussing questions, such as the following:

- How did you know that your card belonged in your group?

- What are some examples of things we push and pull?

Evaluate/Create

13. Provide dominoes to groups of students. Show students how to set up the dominoes one in front of the other. Have students create patterns they can set the dominoes up in so that they will knock each other down.

14. Have students knock down the dominoes.

15. Ask students to explain if they were pushing or pulling to knock the dominoes down. Have students model how they can pull on the dominoes.

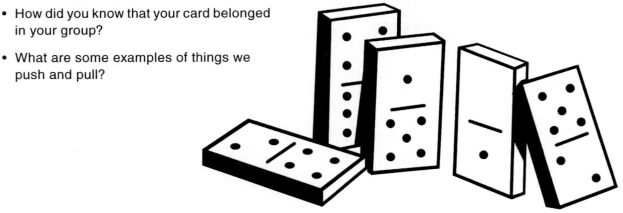

Push and Pull Title Cards

Teacher Directions: Cut apart the cards below.

push

pull

Push and Pull Picture Cards

Teacher Directions: Cut apart the cards below.

Push and Pull Picture Cards *(cont.)*

Push and Pull Picture Cards *(cont.)*

#51184—*Brain-Powered Lessons to Engage All Learners*

Then and Now

Brain-Powered Strategy	Standard
Kinesthetic Word Webs	Understands changes in community over time

Vocabulary Words

- ink
- long ago
- quill
- today

Materials

- *Then and Now Title Cards* (page 92)
- *Then and Now Picture Cards* (pages 93–95)
- photograph of you as a child (*optional*)
- book about life long ago (e.g., *Long Ago and Today* by Rozanne Lanczak Williams)
- photographs of objects from long ago
- drawing paper
- feathers
- black paint

Preparation Note: Prior to the lesson, cut apart the *Then and Now Title Cards* (page 92) and the *Then and Now Picture Cards* (pages 93–95). Have enough available so each student can have one card. You may have more than one copy of the same picture if needed.

Procedures

Model

1. Show students the photograph of you as a child. Explain that many things have changed since you were a child. Share some of the changes you have seen in your lifetime.

2. Reinforce the idea that things change over time by reading a book about long ago.

3. Ask students to think of all the different things they use to write (e.g., pens, pencils, computer). Explain that long ago, people did not have computers or pens and that they used feathers, called quills, dipped in ink to write.

4. Ask students to identify other ways things have changed either from the book you read or from their prior knowledge. Provide examples from your own personal life. Show students photographs or images from the Internet of other objects from long ago.

Then and Now *(cont.)*

Apply/Analyze

5. Tell students that they will be doing a strategy called *Kinesthetic Word Webs*. (For detailed information on this strategy, see page 14.)

6. Provide students with the *Then and Now Title Cards* and the *Then and Now Picture Cards*.

7. Instruct students to walk around the room and form groups to show things from long ago and things from today.

8. Once a group of students thinks their web is complete, instruct them to form an outer circle and have the student holding the title card stand in the middle. The outer circle of students each places one hand on the shoulder of the student with the title card, creating a *Kinesthetic Word Web*.

Evaluate/Create

9. Have students name the items in their groups aloud.

10. Debrief with students by discussing questions, such as the following:

- How did you know if the item was from long ago or from today?

- Do you think someone would want to use an item from the past today?

11. Challenge students to rearrange themselves so they match the modern day equivalent to the item from long ago instead of with other items that are from the same time period.

12. Provide students with drawing paper, feathers, and black paint.

13. Tell students that one thing that has changed since long ago is how we write. Show students how to use the feather and dip it into the black paint to use as a writing tool on the drawing paper. Ask students to write the alphabet using the feather.

Then and Now Title Cards

Teacher Directions: Cut apart the cards below.

Long Ago

Today

Then and Now Picture Cards

Teacher Directions: Cut apart the cards below.

scrub board and tub

washing machine

quill and ink pot

computer

Then and Now Picture Cards (cont.)

horse and carriage

car

clothes

clothes

Then and Now Picture Cards *(cont.)*

telephone

cell phone

fire

stove

Text Types

Brain-Powered Strategy	Standard
Matchmaker	Recognize common types of texts

Vocabulary Words

- fairy tale
- informational
- poem
- storybook
- text type

Materials

- *Text Type Picture Cards* (pages 98–100)
- *Text Type Word Cards* (page 101)
- chart paper
- variety of texts including fairy tales, nursery rhymes, songs, poems, storybooks, and informational books
- tape
- drawing paper
- crayons or markers

Preparation Note: Prior to the lesson, divide a sheet of chart paper into six sections. Label each section with the following words, one word per section: *fairy tale, nursery rhyme, poem, song, informational text*, and *storybook*. Additionally, cut apart the *Text Type Picture Cards* (pages 98–100) and the *Text Type Word Cards* (page 101). An alternative to using the picture cards is to use actual pieces of text that correspond to the word cards. Ensure students have been exposed to a variety of text types leading up to this lesson.

Procedures

Model

1. Display the previously prepared chart paper. Tell students that they will name the features of different types of texts.

2. Read aloud a section of the selected fairy tale.

3. Ask students to identify features of a fairy tale. Guide students' answers to create an accurate description of a fairy tale. Draw and write features named under the section of the chart for fairy tales.

4. Repeat Steps 2–3, modeling other text types.

Apply/Analyze

5. Tell students that they will be doing a strategy called *Matchmaker*. (For detailed information on this strategy, see page 15.)

6. Distribute the *Text Type Word Cards* to students. Help students attach the cards to their shirts using tape.

7. Divide students into groups of five to six. Have students stand in a circle. Place the *Text Type Picture Cards* (or actual texts) on the floor in the center of the circle.

Text Types *(cont.)*

8. Ask students to pick up the picture cards from the center of the circle but not their own card.

9. Have students hold hands around the circle as they also hold the card they picked up. Students must get the picture card to the person wearing the matching word card without letting go of their hands.

10. Allow students to not hold hands if needed. However, the energy level and engagement level increases with the challenge of holding hands and moving the cards around the circle.

11. Have students read the words aloud and show the matching picture cards once they have matched all of the cards. The rest of the group can agree or disagree and, if needed, move the cards to the correct person.

Evaluate/Create

12. Distribute drawing paper to students. Ask students to choose their favorite text types. Students should create covers for books using that text type.

13. Allow students to share their book covers with the rest of the class. Have the rest of the class guess what text type the book is and justify why they think that.

14. Play *Matchmaker* again using the students' book covers as the picture cards to be matched to the word cards.

Text Type Picture Cards

Teacher Directions: Cut apart the cards below.

Roses are red.

Violets are blue.

My secret is that

I love you!

Text Type Picture Cards *(cont.)*

Humpty Dumpty
sat on a wall,

Humpty Dumpty
had a great fall.

Text Type Picture Cards *(cont.)*

Text Type Word Cards

Teacher Directions: Cut apart the cards below.

fairy tale	**poem**
nursery rhyme	**informational book**
storybook	**song**

Get Detailed

Brain-Powered Strategy	Standard
Matchmaker	Use a combination of drawing, dictating, and writing to compose informative/explanatory texts in which they name what they are writing about and supply some information about the topic

Vocabulary Words

- detail
- informational
- topic

Materials

- *Topic and Detail Cards* (pages 104–111)
- easy informational book (e.g., *Seahorses* by Nick Course)
- chart paper
- tape
- writing paper

Preparation Note: Prior to the lesson, cut apart the *Topic and Detail Cards* (pages 104–111).

Procedures

Model

1. Read the title of the selected informational book to students. Tell students that usually the title tells the topic of the book. Explain that all the information in the book will be about the topic.

2. Read aloud the book to students. Stop throughout the book as needed to reinforce that each sentence in the book gives details about the topic.

3. Explain to students that they, too, can write informational text about a topic. Tell students that you will model how to write an informational text about bears.

4. Model writing the topic sentence on the sheet of chart paper. The topic can be as simple or elaborate as needed for your students. For example: *Bears are animals. Bears are mammals that are found on five continents.*

5. Tell students that since bears are your topic, every sentence that follows must be about bears. No other topic can be introduced.

6. Model adding detail sentences to support the topic of bears. Reinforce that each sentence tells about bears.

7. Read the completed paragraph. Stop after each sentence and remind students that it tells about the topic.

Get Detailed *(cont.)*

Apply/Analyze

8. Tell students that they will be doing a strategy called *Matchmaker*. (For detailed information on this strategy, see page 15.)

9. Distribute a *Topic and Detail Card* to each student. Help students attach their cards to their shirts using tape.

10. Divide students into small groups of five to eight. Have each group of students stand in a circle. Place the detail cards with the sentences on the floor randomly in the center of the circle.

11. Ask students to pick up the sentence cards from the center of their circle but not their own card.

12. Have students hold hands around the circle as they also hold the card they picked up. Students must get the sentence card to the person wearing the matching word card without letting go of their hands. Allow students to help each other read the sentence cards, or you can read the sentences aloud if needed.

13. Allow students to not hold hands if needed. However, the energy level and engagement level increases with the challenge of holding hands and moving the cards around the circle.

14. Have students read the topic and the matching detail sentence aloud once they have matched all the cards. The rest of the group can agree or disagree and, if needed, move the cards to the correct person.

Evaluate/Create

15. Distribute writing paper to students. Have them write one additional detail sentence to match the topic card they had during the activity.

16. Gather students together again. Have each student read aloud his or her topic, the detail sentence from the activity, and the sentence they wrote. Ask students to explain how the sentences they wrote support the topic sentences.

Topic and Detail Cards

Teacher Directions: Cut apart the cards below.

dog

Dogs can smell well.

Topic and Detail Cards *(cont.)*

car

A car needs a driver.

Topic and Detail Cards *(cont.)*

dinosaur

Dinosaurs lived long ago.

Topic and Detail Cards *(cont.)*

computer

Keyboards help people type words on computers.

Topic and Detail Cards *(cont.)*

horse

Horses can run fast.

Topic and Detail Cards *(cont.)*

school

Teachers teach at schools.

Topic and Detail Cards *(cont.)*

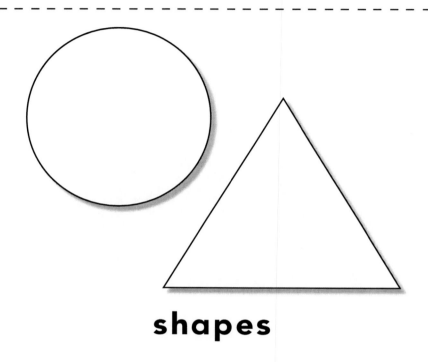

shapes

Triangles have 3 sides.

Topic and Detail Cards *(cont.)*

space

The sun is a star.

Wonderful Weather

Brain-Powered Strategy	Standard
Matchmaker	Knows vocabulary for different types of weather

Vocabulary Words

- cloudy
- rainy
- snowy
- sunny
- windy

Materials

- *Weather Picture Cards* (page 114)
- *Weather Word Cards* (pages 115–117)
- chart paper
- tape
- drawing paper
- crayons or markers

Preparation Note: Prior to the lesson, cut apart the *Weather Picture Cards* (page 114) and the *Weather Word Cards* (pages 115–117).

Procedures

Model

1. Engage students with the lesson by singing and doing the hand motions for "The Itsy Bitsy Spider."

2. Have students name the types of weather that are named in the song.

3. Take students on a quick field trip outside to look at the weather. Help students discuss what they observe. Ask questions such as, "What does the sky look like?" Return to the classroom.

4. Use hand motions to pantomime the various types of weather. For example:

sunny	hold hands in a circle above your head to represent a sun
rainy	wiggle your fingers in front of you from just above your head down to your waist
windy	blow air out of your mouth, and move hands quickly from side to side
cloudy	use your hands to make bumps in the air to represent clouds
snowy	wiggle your fingers in front of you as you move your hands from side to side

Wonderful Weather *(cont.)*

5. Draw a quick picture of each type of weather on a sheet of chart paper. Label each picture.

6. Ask students to name any other types of weather they are familiar with. Add any additional types of weather to the chart that students did not name.

Apply/Analyze

7. Tell students that they will be doing a strategy called *Matchmaker*. (For detailed information on this strategy, see page 15.)

8. Distribute the *Weather Picture Cards* to students. Help students attach their cards to their shirts using tape.

9. Have students stand in a circle. Place the *Weather Word Cards* on the floor randomly in the center of the circle.

10. Ask students to pick up the cards from the center of the circle but not their own card.

11. Have students hold hands around the circle as they also hold the card they picked up. Students must get the word card to the person wearing the matching picture card without letting go of their hands.

12. Allow students to not hold hands if needed. However, the energy level and engagement level increases with the challenge of holding hands and moving the cards around the circle.

13. Have students read the words aloud and show the matching picture cards once they have matched all the cards. The rest of the group can agree or disagree and, if needed, move the cards to the correct person.

Evaluate/Create

14. Distribute drawing paper to students. Have them choose their favorite types of weather and draw pictures of themselves in that type of weather. Encourage students to draw clothing appropriate to that type of weather. Have students label the pictures or write sentences to match the pictures.

15. Have students share their pictures with a partner. Ask them to explain to one another why they made the choice of clothing they did. Have partners work together to think of other clothing that would be appropriate/not appropriate for the weather.

Weather Picture Cards

Teacher Directions: Cut apart the cards below.

Weather Word Cards

Teacher Directions: Cut apart the cards below.

sunny

cloudy

Weather Word Cards *(cont.)*

rainy

snowy

Weather Word Cards *(cont.)*

windy

Community Workers

Brain-Powered Strategy	Standard
Matchmaker	Knows how different groups of people in the community have taken responsibility for the common good

Vocabulary Words

- community
- occupation
- past
- present
- tool

Materials

- *Community Worker Picture Cards* (pages 120–121)
- *Tool Picture Cards* (pages 122–125)
- chart paper
- tape
- drawing/writing paper
- crayons or markers

Preparation Note: Prior to the lesson, cut apart the *Community Worker Picture Cards* (pages 120–121) and the *Tool Picture Cards* (pages 122–125). Also, divide chart paper into two columns. Label the column on the left *Workers* and the column on the right *Tools*.

Procedures

Model

1. Recite the poem "Rub-a-Dub-Dub" with students:

   Rub-a-dub-dub,
   Three men in a tub,
   And who do you think they be?
   The butcher, the baker, the candlestick maker,
   And all of them turned out to sea.

2. Discuss with students the occupations of the three men in the tub. Ask students to identify where each of those men would work.

3. Tell students there are many workers in the community that they are already familiar with. Provide the clues below. Have students work with partners to try to name each worker. Provide additional clues if students are unable to determine the correct worker. Record student responses on the sheet of chart paper.

   - This person helps keep you healthy.
   - This person teaches children.
   - This person flies people places.
   - This person helps put out fires.
   - This person keeps the community safe.
   - This person brings mail to people.
   - This person bakes bread for people to buy.
   - This person helps people with their money.

Community Workers *(cont.)*

4. Name each worker, one at a time. Have students turn to partners and share any tools they know about that the worker needs to do his or her job. Have students share their ideas aloud. Record them on the chart paper in the corresponding column.

Apply/Analyze

5. Tell students they will be doing a strategy called *Matchmaker*. (For detailed information on this strategy, see page 15.)

6. Provide each student with a *Community Worker Picture Card*. Help students attach their cards to their shirts using tape.

7. Have students stand in a circle. Place the *Tool Picture Cards* on the floor randomly in the center of the circle.

8. Ask students to pick up the cards from the center of the circle but not their own card.

9. Have students hold hands around the circle as they also hold the card they picked up. Students must get the tool picture card to the person wearing the matching helper picture card without letting go of their hands.

10. Allow students to not hold hands if needed. However, the energy level and engagement level increases with the challenge of holding hands and moving the cards around the circle.

11. Have students share aloud the community helper and the corresponding tool the helper uses once all the cards have been matched. The rest of the group can agree or disagree and, if needed, move the cards to the correct person.

Evaluate/Create

12. Distribute drawing paper with lines for students to write. Ask students to draw and write about what kind of workers they would like to be when they grow up. Allow time for students to work.

13. Have students share the job they want to be with partners. Ask them to explain at least one reason why they chose what they want to be when they grow up.

14. Have students share their writing with partners. Then, select a few volunteers to share with the whole class.

Community Worker Picture Cards

Teacher Directions: Cut apart the cards below.

Community Worker Picture Cards *(cont.)*

Tool Picture Cards

Teacher Directions: Cut apart the cards below.

#51184—Brain-Powered Lessons to Engage All Learners   © *Shell Education*

Tool Picture Cards *(cont.)*

Tool Picture Cards *(cont.)*

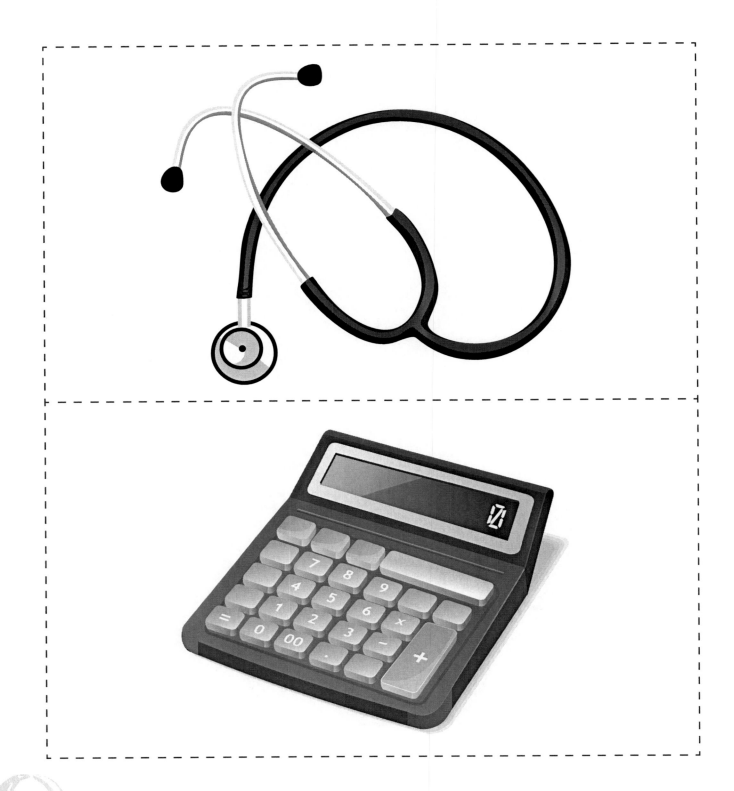

Tool Picture Cards *(cont.)*

Story Retell

Brain-Powered Strategy	Standard
Reverse, Reverse!	With prompting and support, retell familiar stories, including key details

Vocabulary Words

- retell
- reverse
- sequence

Materials

- selected piece of literature
- chart paper
- index cards
- crayons or markers

Procedures

Model

1. Preview a piece of literature by taking a picture walk through the book. Encourage students to discuss the illustrations as you preview the book.

2. Read the piece of literature to students. Stop throughout the story to discuss what is happening or to clarify anything that students may need assistance understanding.

3. Explain to students that one way to show they understand a story is to tell the story in their own words. Tell students that this is called a *retell*.

4. Tell students that a good retell of a story includes several items. Review each of the following items as you list it on chart paper:

   - the names of characters
   - the setting of the story
   - the events of the story in the correct sequence—beginning, middle, and end

5. Model retelling the story you read to students in Step 2. Point to each item on the chart paper as you include it in your retell.

Story Retell *(cont.)*

Apply/Analyze

6. Tell students they will be doing a strategy called *Reverse, Reverse!* (For detailed information on this strategy, see page 16.)

7. Gather students together to form a circle. Select one student to be the judge, or you can be the judge.

8. Have the first student begin retelling the story. The student should only say one sentence that begins the story. Continue having students retell the story by adding one sentence each in a clockwise direction around the circle. The next student says a sentence that continues the story, and so on. If a student makes a mistake in the sequence of the story or misses a key detail, reverse the direction so the direction is now counterclockwise.

9. Play continues until the story has been completely retold.

Evaluate/Create

10. Distribute index cards to students. Have students work individually or with partners to retell the story with illustrations. Each part of the story can be placed on one index card. Then, have students place the index cards in the order the events occurred to retell the story.

11. Monitor students' understanding of the story. Once they have been able to demonstrate a good understanding of the sequence of events, ask them to discuss with partners how the story would change if one of the characters was not in the story or if the setting of the story was different.

12. Group pairs of students together, and have the partners share with each other what they discussed, or allow several pairs to share aloud with the whole class.

Counting

Brain-Powered Strategy	Standard
Reverse, Reverse!	Count to 100 by ones and by tens

Vocabulary Words	Materials
• counting • ones • reverse • tens	• *Counting Mat* (pages 130–131)

Procedures

Model

1. Draw a number line from 1 to 10 on the board. Have students practice counting to 10 aloud with you. Point to the numbers on the number line as students say them.

2. Practice counting to 10 several more times. Each time, have students use a different voice such as a baby voice, an opera voice, or a papa bear voice.

3. Ask students what number comes after 10. Tell students that before they can continue to count, you have to add on to the number line.

4. Extend the number line and add more numbers to it. As you add numbers to the number line, say the number aloud. Have students repeat the numbers as you say them. Continue the number line until a designated stopping point, which will vary by class and time of year.

5. Have students practice counting aloud to 20 on the number line as you point to each number. Practice several times using various voices as suggested in Step 2.

6. Choose a number in the middle of the number line. Have students practice counting forward from that number. Point to the numbers on the number line to provide support as needed.

Apply/Analyze

7. Tell students they will be doing a strategy called *Reverse, Reverse!* (For detailed information on this strategy, see page 16.)

8. Gather students together to form a circle. Select one student to be the judge, or you can be the judge.

Counting *(cont.)*

9. Have the first student begin counting at one (or any other number you designate). Continue having students count in a clockwise direction. The next student says the next number, and so on. If a student makes a mistake in the number sequence, reverse the direction so the direction is now counterclockwise.

10. Have students repeat the activity, but this time, counting by 10s.

11. Play continues until a predetermined amount of time, number of times around the circle, or a specific number is reached in counting (e.g., 100) has been met.

Evaluate/Create

12. Distribute the *Counting Mat* activity sheet (pages 130–131) to students. Have them draw one apple in each box. Then, have them practice counting the apples.

13. Group students into pairs or triads. Have students look at their *Counting Mats* and describe what is happening as they are counting. For example, students could say the numbers are getting bigger or they are adding one each time they count. Ask students to use the mat to count backward. Have them describe what is happening as they count backward.

Name: _____   Date: _____

Counting Mat

Directions: Draw one apple in each box. Practice counting the apples.

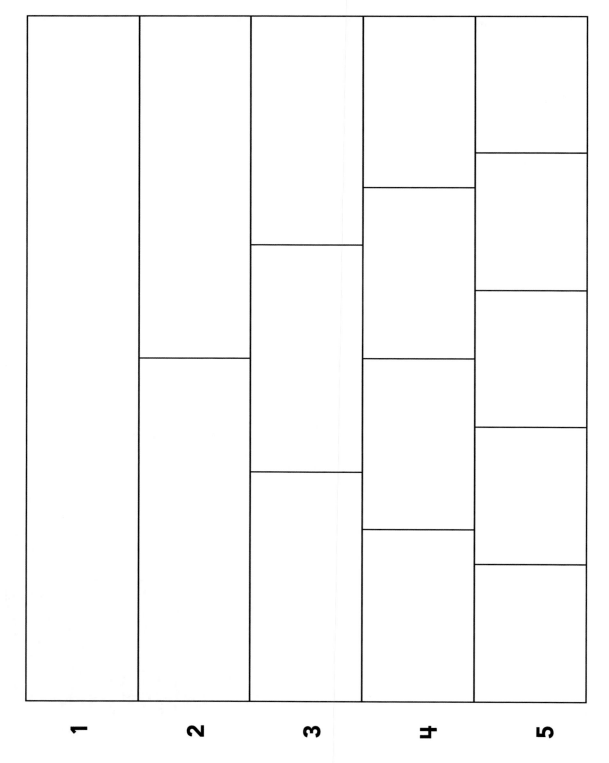

1   2   3   4   5

Name: _____   Date: _____

Counting Mat (cont.)

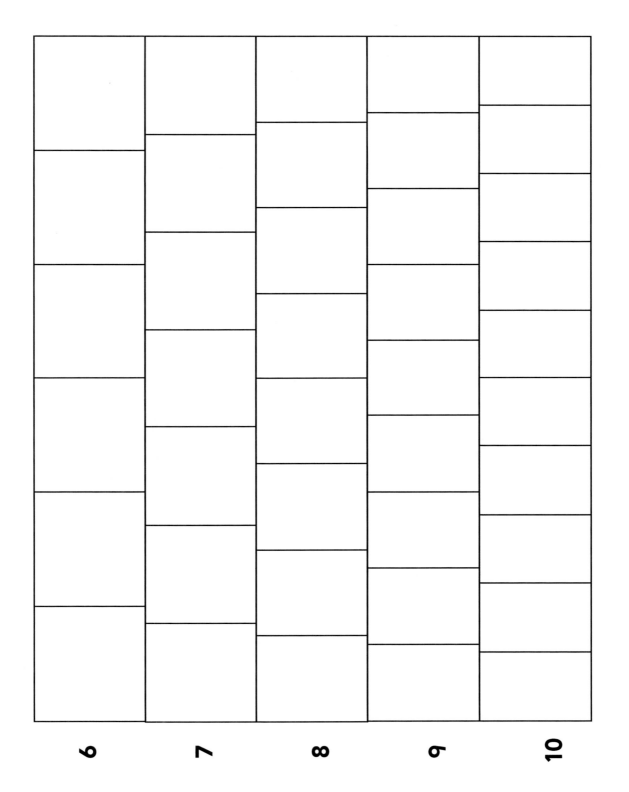

6   7   8   9   10

Favorite Character

Brain-Powered Strategy	Standard
Show It with Dough!	Use a combination of drawings, dictating, and writing to compose opinion pieces in which they tell a reader the topic or name of the book they are writing about and state an opinion or preference about the topic or book

Vocabulary Words

- character
- favorite
- opinion
- topic

Materials

- *No-Cook Dough Recipe* (page 134)
- *Favorite Character Writing Paper* (page 135)
- storybook with strong characters
- chart paper
- crayons

Preparation Note: Prior to the lesson, create molding dough for students using the *No-Cook Dough Recipe* (page 134).

Procedures

Model

1. Ask students to raise their hands if they like the following fruits:

   - apples
   - bananas
   - strawberries
   - watermelon

2. Tell students that although many people like those fruits, if they have to choose their favorite, they can only choose one.

3. Name the fruits again, one at a time. Ask students to raise their hands only one time to show the fruit that is their favorite.

4. Explain that the one they chose as their favorite is their opinion because not everyone will agree with them. Ask students who chose different favorite fruits to share their reasons for choosing the fruit they did.

Favorite Character *(cont.)*

5. Display and discuss the cover of the storybook you will read to students. Explain to students that there are many characters in the story and they will have to decide at the end of the story which character is their favorite.

6. Read the book to students, stopping as needed to discuss the plot and characters.

7. Ask students to name the characters from the story. Write the characters' names on a sheet of chart paper. Display the chart paper so students can reference it during the rest of the lesson.

Apply/Analyze

8. Tell students that they will be doing a strategy called *Show It with Dough!* (For detailed information on this strategy, see page 17.)

9. Provide students with portions of dough.

10. Have students create the character they liked the best out of the dough. Provide students time to work. As they work, encourage them to create other items that may tell about why the character was their favorite. For example, if the character was their favorite because she picked flowers, students may create a flower to put in the character's hand.

11. Have students share with a partner which characters they created and why.

12. Ask for volunteers or select several students to share with the whole class about their dough characters.

Evaluate/Create

13. Distribute the *Favorite Character Writing Paper* activity sheet (page 135) to students. Ask students to draw and write about their favorite character from the book and why that character was their favorite. You may wish to provide the following sentence frame as writing support: *My favorite character is _____ because _____.*

14. Allow students to keep their dough character on their desks, and remind them to think about their dough figure as they write.

15. Provide time for students to share their writing with the same partners they worked with in Step 11. Encourage partners to provide feedback about whether what was shared in Step 11 and what was written about matched.

No-Cook Dough Recipe

Teacher Directions: Use the recipe below to make dough.

Ingredients

- ☑ 1 cup flour
- ☑ $\frac{3}{8}$ cup salt
- ☑ $\frac{3}{8}$ cup hot tap water
- ☑ food coloring *(optional)*

Steps

1. Combine the flour and salt in a medium-sized bowl.

2. Pour in the hot water and stir well.

3. Knead the dough for at least five minutes, working in food coloring if desired.

Note: Depending on the thickness of the dough, air-drying can take between one and five days. The dough will keep for up to a week when refrigerated in plastic bags or sealed containers.

Name: _____   Date: _____

Favorite Character Writing Paper

Directions: Draw and write an answer to the question.

[drawing box]

Who was your favorite character and why?

_____

- -

_____

- -

_____

Give Me Ten

Brain-Powered Strategy	Standard
Show It with Dough!	Decompose numbers less than or equal to 10 into pairs in more than one way

Vocabulary Words

- addition
- equation

Materials

- *No-Cook Dough Recipe* (page 134); two colors of dough
- *Ten Frames Work Mat* (page 138)
- *12 Ways to Get to 11* by Eve Merriam (or other mathematical book on decomposing numbers)
- index cards
- crayons

Preparation Note: Prior to the lesson, create molding dough for students using the *No-Cook Dough Recipe* (page 134). Divide the dough into enough portions for each student to have some of each color. Additionally, write the numbers 0, 1, 2, 3, 4, and 5 on individual index cards.

Procedures

Model

1. Read the selected book to introduce the concept of decomposing numbers.

2. Have students help write equations to match each picture in the book.

3. Line up five students at the front of the room. Explain that the same five students can be grouped in different ways.

4. Rearrange the five students to model the following groupings: 5 and 0, 4 and 1, and 3 and 2. Have the groups hold up the previously made index cards with the numbers that correspond to the number of people in their groups.

5. Repeat Step 4, this time modeling how to write an addition equation to match the groupings.

Apply/Analyze

6. Tell students that they will be doing a strategy called *Show It with Dough!* (For detailed information on this strategy, see page 17.)

7. Distribute two different colors of dough and the *Ten Frames Work Mat* activity sheet (page 138) to students.

Give Me Ten *(cont.)*

8. Have students make 10 small balls out of each color of dough for a total of 20 balls.

9. Ask students to choose 10 of the balls of any color and place one ball in each of the boxes of a ten frame on their work mat.

10. Have students share aloud the number of each color they used. Record the responses on the board. Discuss with students why there are so many different ways to make 10.

11. Have students take one ball of dough off the work mat at a time and color a circle with the corresponding color so the dough model is recorded in crayon.

12. Provide time for students to complete the second ten frame with different pairings of colors of dough.

Evaluate/Create

13. Write an addition equation on the board with a sum of less than 10.

14. Create two dough models on ten frames. One model should accurately represent the equation. The other model should not accurately represent the equation.

15. Display both models so students can see them. Have students discuss with partners which ten frame accurately models the equation and why.

16. Have students share their responses and rationale aloud.

Name: _____   Date: _____

Ten Frames Work Mat

Directions: Use dough to show different ways to fill the ten frames.

1   **2**

Where Is It?

Brain-Powered Strategy	**Standard**
Show It with Dough!	Knows that the position of an object can be described by locating it relative to another object or the background

Vocabulary Words

- behind
- in front of
- location
- next to
- position

Materials

- *No-Cook Dough Recipe* (page 134); two colors of dough
- drawing paper or cardboard
- index cards
- small prizes or candy

Preparation Note: Prior to the lesson, create molding dough for students using the *No-Cook Dough Recipe* (page 134). Divide the dough into enough portions for each student to have some of each color.

Procedures

Model

1. Ask students where they are. Entertain all ideas at this point.

2. Explain to students that location (or where an object is) can be described by the position an object is in.

3. Stand in the front of the classroom. Have students stand at their desks facing you. Tell students you are located in front of the class. Write the following sentence frame on the board: _____ *is in front of* _____.

4. Assist students in completing the sentence, and then practice it orally several times with students.

5. Have students practice both modeling the position with other students and the sentence frame.

6. Repeat Steps 3–5 several more times modeling different positions. **Note:** Only model three or four different positions during each lesson. Repeat the lesson using different positions as needed.

Where Is It? *(cont.)*

Apply/Analyze

7. Tell students that they will be doing a strategy called *Show It with Dough!* (For detailed information on this strategy, see page 17.)

8. Distribute a sheet of drawing paper or a piece of cardboard to students, as well as the dough. Ask students to shape each color of dough into a ball.

9. Tell students to place one color of dough at the top of the drawing paper and the other color at the bottom. Write the following sentence frame on the board: *The _____ ball is in front of the _____ ball.* Keep sentence frames listed on the board for students to reference throughout the lesson.

10. Assist students in completing the sentence frame and have students read it with you.

11. Continue providing students with other directions using words such as *behind* and *next to* in order to have them practice positioning the dough balls. Provide sentence frames for students to practice orally explaining the positions of the dough balls. Include other locations as students have shown mastery of locations already introduced.

Evaluate/Create

12. Divide students into groups of four to five. Distribute an index card to each student. Have groups work together to create treasure hunts using the position words that are being practiced. Place the vocabulary words from the lesson on the board. You may wish to include sentence frames as well. Students can reference the words and sentence frames, and draw pictures of any other objects. For example, students can write: Look *beside* the _____. Each person in the group should create one card.

13. Assist groups in placing their index cards in the correct places around the room, so that one card leads to another card. Place small prizes or candy in an ending location. Have other groups follow the clues to find the treasure.

14. Gather students back together. Discuss which clues were easiest/most difficult to follow. Help students evaluate which words are more precise to use in various situations, for example: *below/under*, *beside/next to*.

Land and Water

Brain-Powered Strategy	Standard
Show It with Dough!	Understands characteristics and uses of maps, globes, and other geographic tools and technologies

Vocabulary Words

- globe
- land
- map
- three-dimensional
- two-dimensional
- water

Materials

- *No-Cook Dough Recipe* (page 134); two colors of dough (blue and green)
- globe
- world map
- index cards
- state map
- cardboard
- crayons

Preparation Note: Prior to the lesson, create molding dough for students using the *No-Cook Dough Recipe* (page 134). Divide the dough into enough portions for each student to have some of each color.

Procedures

Model

1. Display a globe. Tell students the globe is a model of Earth. Spin the globe so they can see all the way around it.

2. Display a world map for students. Tell students that a map is a flat version of a globe. Explain that since the globe is three-dimensional, it is difficult to carry around. Tell students that a map is two-dimensional or flat and it is much easier to carry around.

3. Show students several easily identifiable locations on the globe and the corresponding location on the map so students can see they show the same location.

4. Point out to students that there are many colors on both globes and maps, and explain that they show the places where there is land and water on Earth. Ask students which color is shown most on the globe (blue). Tell them the blue represents the water. Show students the large areas of water (oceans).

Land and Water *(cont.)*

5. Tell students the other colors represent the land (usually brown or green). Point out the various continents to students, including where on Earth you live.

6. Point to the blue features on the map, and ask students to brainstorm what they think the features are. Show students that there are some water (blue) features on the land. Tell students these show water features such as lakes and rivers. Draw some of the water features on the board, if needed, so students can see that rivers are usually a long, thin shape and lakes usually have a fuller shape.

Apply/Analyze

7. Tell students that they will be doing a strategy called *Show It with Dough!* (For detailed information on this strategy, see page 17.)

8. Distribute the dough and index cards to students. Have students draw the shape of the state in which they live on the card.

9. Display a more detailed state map. Have students use green dough to show land features of the state on their index cards. Have students use blue dough to show water features of the state on their index cards.

Evaluate/Create

10. Provide students with a piece of cardboard. Allow them time to create imaginary maps that include land and water features on them. Have students label the geographic features by writing *land* and *water* and drawing arrows to where they placed them on the maps.

11. Place an index card in front of each model. Have students stand up and rotate one student to the left. On the index card, have students draw what they see on the model. Rotate around the room reviewing the maps students are drawing in order to evaluate student progress with the lesson concept. Take anecdotal notes as needed.

12. Have students work with partners to determine if they live close to any water features that were discussed in Step 6 of the lesson. For example, students could say they live close to a lake.

Add Details

Brain-Powered Strategy	Standard
I'm in the Pic	With guidance and support from adults, respond to questions and suggestions from peers and add details to strengthen writing as needed
Vocabulary Words • details	**Materials** • *By the Ocean* (page 145) • *Ocean Writing* (page 146) • *I'm in the Picture* (page 147)

Procedures

Model

1. Ask students to share any previous experiences with the ocean.

2. Display the *By the Ocean* photograph (page 145). You may wish to use a real beach image found on the Digital Resource CD (bytheocean.pdf). Distribute the *Ocean Writing* activity sheet (page 146) to students. Have students write one sentence about the photograph next to the number one. Ask students to set aside their writing papers for later use.

3. Ask students to take another look at the photograph *By the Ocean*. Explain that by pretending to be in the picture, students can find specific details to help them make their writing better.

4. Ask students the following question, "If you were in this picture, what might you see?"

5. Model for students naming several things you either see in the picture or might see if you were in the picture.

6. Ask students to share their more detailed observations of the picture or their ideas of what they might be able to see in the picture.

Apply/Analyze

7. Tell students that they will be doing a strategy called *I'm in the Pic*. (For detailed information on this strategy, see page 18.)

8. Divide students into pairs or groups of three. Distribute the *I'm in the Picture* activity sheet (page 147) and the *By the Ocean* activity sheet (page 145) to each student.

9. Ask students the following questions to get them thinking more deeply about the photograph:

   • What might you touch?
   • What might you hear?
   • What could you possibly smell?
   • What might you taste if you went for a swim in the ocean?
   • How might you feel if you were in the picture?

Add Details *(cont.)*

10. Allow students to complete the activity sheet. Then, lead a discussion with students about their findings.

Evaluate/Create

11. Have students retrieve their *Ocean Writing* activity sheet. Have students fold their papers so they cannot see the sentence they previously wrote.

12. Ask students to write a new sentence about the ocean photograph using some of the details they recorded on the *I'm in the Picture* activity sheet.

13. Have students review the sentences they wrote, and identify which senses they used when writing the second sentence.

14. Ask students to discuss in pairs which sense is the most important to use when describing the ocean to someone and why. Allow several students to share their thoughts aloud.

#51184—*Brain-Powered Lessons to Engage All Learners*   © *Shell Education*

Name: _____ Date: _____

By the Ocean

Directions: Look at the picture below. Use the picture to complete the *I'm in the Picture* activity sheet.

Name: _____ **Date:** _____

Ocean Writing

Directions: Write about the photograph *By the Ocean.*

Sentence 1

1. _____
   - - - - - - - - - - - - - - - - - - -
   _____
   - - - - - - - - - - - - - - - - - - -
   _____
   - - - - - - - - - - - - - - - - - - -
   _____

Sentence 2

2. _____
   - - - - - - - - - - - - - - - - - - -
   _____
   - - - - - - - - - - - - - - - - - - -
   _____
   - - - - - - - - - - - - - - - - - - -
   _____

Name: _____   Date: _____

I'm in the Picture

Directions: Look at the picture *By the Ocean*. Write or draw details from the picture in each box below.

I'm in the Picture!	I smell...
I see...	I taste...
I hear...	I touch...

What Was It Like?

Brain-Powered Strategy	Standard
I'm in the Pic	Understands family life today and how it compares with family life in the recent past and family life long ago

Vocabulary Words	Materials
• long ago • one-room school house	• *I'm in the Picture* (page 150) • *One-Room School House* (page 151) • chart paper • drawing paper

Preparation Note: Divide a sheet of chart paper into six boxes. Write the word *school* in the first box and then each of the five senses in the remaining boxes.

Procedures

Model

1. Tell students that today they will talk about something they know lots about—school.

2. Ask students to discuss with a partner their favorite things about school.

3. Tell students to think about their classroom. Provide them time to look around the classroom.

4. Ask students questions that will guide their responses. Record their descriptions in the appropriate boxes (you may wish to use pictures) on the chart paper in order to model for students how they will complete their activity sheets. Ask students the following questions:

   • What do you see?

   • What can you touch?

   • What do you smell?

   • What do you hear?

   • Do you ever taste anything at school?

What Was It Like? *(cont.)*

Apply/Analyze

5. Tell students that they will be doing a strategy called *I'm in the Pic*. (For detailed information on this strategy, see page 18.)

6. Divide students into pairs or groups. Distribute a copy of the *I'm in the Picture* activity sheet (page 150) and the *One-Room School House* photograph. You may wish to use a real school image found on the Digital Resource CD (oneroomschoolhouse.pdf) (page 151) to each student. Tell students that schools long ago only had one room—for the whole school!

7. Allow students to complete the activity sheet. Then, lead a discussion with students about how they feel their lives would be different if they lived during the time of one-room school houses.

Evaluate/Create

8. Provide students with drawing paper. Have students fold the drawing paper in half.

9. Ask students to choose something from the way schools were long ago and draw it on the left side of the paper and the corresponding modern-day item on the right side of the paper. For example, students could draw an inkpot on the left and a pencil or pen on the right.

10. Have students share their drawings with the class. Once each student has shared, divide students into groups of three. Have each triad determine what from schools long ago is the most/least similar to schools today. Provide time for each triad to share its choice and why.

Name: _____ **Date:** _____

I'm in the Picture

Directions: Look at the picture *One-Room School House.* Write or draw details from the picture in each box below.

I'm in the Picture!	I smell...
I see...	I taste...
I hear...	I touch...

  © Shell Education

Name: _____ Date: _____

One-Room School House

Directions: Look at the picture below. Use the picture to complete the *I'm in the Picture* activity sheet.

So, What Do You Think?

Brain-Powered Strategy	Standard
Just Say It	With guidance and support from adults, respond to questions and suggestions from peers and add details to strengthen writing as needed

Vocabulary Words

- details
- respond
- strengthen
- suggestions

Materials

- chart paper
- first draft of writing (see Preparation Note below)

Preparation Note: Prior to the lesson, have students write a first draft on any topic of the teacher or students' choosing.

Procedures

Model

1. Draw a quick picture on a sheet of chart paper of a stick figure and one tree. Tell students that this is a picture of you at the park.

2. Explain to students that this is just your first attempt at drawing the park picture and you know they have a lot of experience at the park they can share to strengthen the picture.

3. Allow students to share aloud more details that should be added to the picture. Draw the details in the picture as students share their ideas.

4. Display the park picture where it can still be seen. Write one simple sentence about the park picture such as *This is me at the park.*

5. Tell students that just like they helped provide suggestions for details that would strengthen the picture, they can also provide suggestions that will strengthen your writing.

6. Remind students that you are very proud of the writing you have already done, so when someone talks about your writing, it should be done in a positive way. Write the following response stems on a separate sheet of chart paper. Tell students these are some stems they can use that will help ensure they are being respectful of their peers:

   - *I like _____.*
   - *What is _____?*
   - *Who is _____?*
   - *I want to know more about _____.*

So, What Do You Think? *(cont.)*

7. Allow students to use some of the stems to provide suggestions for strengthening your writing.

8. Revise your writing based on students' suggestions.

Apply/Analyze

9. Tell students that they will be using a strategy called *Just Say It*. (For detailed information on this strategy, see page 19.)

10. Divide students into pairs. Have the two students face each other and identify one as Partner *A* and the other as Partner *B*.

11. Have Partner *A* share his or her writing with Partner *B*.

12. Provide Partner *B* 30 seconds to respond to the writing of Partner *A*. Encourage students to use the response stems that are listed on the chart paper. Partner *A* should listen attentively.

13. Have partners switch roles and allow Partner *B* to share his or her writing and Partner *A* to respond.

Evaluate/Create

14. Have students return to their desks to work on revising their writing based on the feedback their partners gave them.

15. Allow partners to come back together to share the revised writing. Ask students to identify which part of the partner's feedback was most helpful to strengthen their writing.

16. Provide time for students to share their completed writing with the whole class.

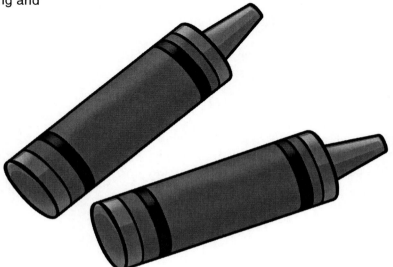

Describe It

Brain-Powered Strategy	Standard
Just Say It	Directly compare two objects with a measurable attribute in common, to see which object has "more of"/"less of" the attribute, and describe the difference

Vocabulary Words	Materials
• attribute • compare • describe • measurable	• variety of objects (e.g., ruler, crayon, pencil) • paper bag • stuffed animal

Preparation Note: Prior to the lesson, gather a variety of objects from the classroom that students can describe. Then, place the objects in a paper bag.

Procedures

Model

1. Hold up the stuffed animal. Ask students to raise their hands if they think the stuffed animal is *tall*. Ask students to raise their hands if they think the stuffed animal is *short*. Point out that some students thought it was tall and others thought it was short.

2. Tell students that when using the words *tall* and *short*, it is useful to compare the objects to another object in order to understand the size.

3. Ask students to look at your height. Reinforce that how tall or short you are depends on what you are being compared to.

4. Walk over to the door. Describe your height in relation to the door. "The door is *taller* than me, or I am *shorter* than the door."

5. Continue to compare yourself to other objects in the classroom. Reinforce other attributes such as weight as well.

6. Have all students in the class stand up. Challenge students to line up at the door from the tallest to the shortest. Write the following sentence frames on the board: _____ *is taller than* _____, *and* _____ *is shorter than* _____.

7. Assist students in completing the sentence frames in order to show direct comparisons.

Describe It *(cont.)*

Apply/Analyze

8. Tell students that they will be using a strategy called *Just Say It*. (For detailed information on this strategy, see page 19.)

9. Divide students into pairs. Have the two students face each other and identify one as Partner *A* and the other as Partner *B*.

10. Rotate around the room with the paper bag of objects, and have each group select two objects from the bag.

11. Provide Partner *A* 30 seconds to compare the two objects. Partner *B* should listen attentively.

12. Have partners switch and allow 30 seconds for Partner *B* to compare the two objects. This time, Partner *A* should listen.

13. Provide Partner *A* additional time for any other insights gained while Partner *B* was speaking.

14. Allow students time to discuss the ideas each of them said.

15. Allow students to trade out the objects they described, and repeat the activity if desired.

Evaluate/Create

16. Combine several groups together. Have the newly formed group combine all the objects they discussed in the previous activity.

17. Have the group choose one attribute to use to describe the objects (e.g., height, weight). Challenge the group to order the objects by that attribute. Allow each group to share aloud how they ordered their objects.

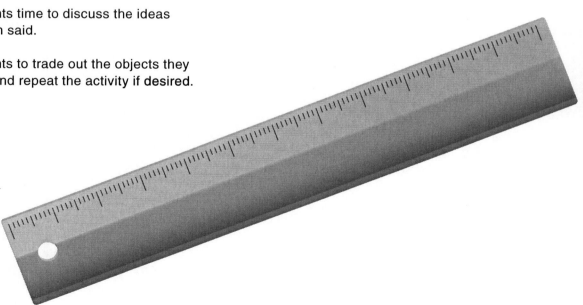

It's In the Community

Brain-Powered Strategy	Standard
Just Say It	Knows the physical and human characteristics of the local community

Vocabulary Words	Materials
• community • local • locations • mural	• butcher paper • index cards • chart paper • mural supplies (e.g., construction paper, paint)

Preparation Note: Prior to the lesson, prepare butcher paper for a community mural. Draw and label major streets or highways in the community. Determine how students will create the mural. For example, will they paint the locations right on the mural or will they draw the locations on construction paper and then cut out and glue the location on the mural, etc.?

Procedures

Model

1. Ask students to name where they are right now (school).

2. Explain that the school is a place in the community, but there are many other places besides the school that are in the community. Explain that a community is the people and locations in a particular area. Name the community in which the school is located.

3. Tell students that they will make a class mural that shows various locations in the local community.

4. Explain to students that the locations they will show include places people live, work, go to school, play, and shop.

5. Ask students to begin thinking about the places in their community by asking them some of the following questions:

   • What parks do you like to go to?

   • Where does your family buy groceries?

   • Where is your school located?

Apply/Analyze

6. Tell students that in order to prepare for the mural, they will be doing a strategy called *Just Say It*. (For detailed information on this strategy, see page 19.)

7. Divide students into pairs. Have the two students face each other and identify one as Partner *A* and the other as Partner *B*.

8. Distribute six to eight index cards to students.

It's In the Community *(cont.)*

9. Provide Partner *A* 30 seconds to list as many places in the community as possible. Partner *B* should listen attentively.

10. Have partners switch and allow 30 seconds for Partner *B* to list places in the community that were not already named. This time, Partner *A* should listen.

11. Provide Partner *A* additional time to name any other locations the student thought of while Partner *B* was speaking.

12. Have students record each location their partners said on an individual index card. Allow students to write or draw to record their ideas.

13. Have students report out the various locations they listed on the recording sheets. Create a master list on a sheet of chart paper that lists all of the locations.

Evaluate/Create

14. Divide students into pairs. Assign each pair a location in the community.

15. Provide students with mural supplies and time to create their assigned location.

16. Assist students in placing their assigned location in the correct place on the mural. Display and discuss the completed mural.

References Cited

Anderson, Lorin and David Krathwohl (Eds.). 2001. "*Taxonomy for Learning, Teaching, and Assessing: A Revision of Bloom's Taxonomy of Educational Objectives.*" Boston, MA: Pearson Education Group.

Bloom, Benjamin (Ed.). 1956. *Taxonomy of Educational Objectives.* New York: David McKay Company.

Covington, Martin V. 2000. "Goal Theory, Motivation, and School Achievement: An Integrative Review." Retrieved from http://ww2.csdm.qc.ca/SaintEmile/bernet/annexes/ASS6826/Covington2000.pdf.

Doidge, Norman. 2007. *The Brain That Changes Itself: Stories of Personal Triumph from the Frontiers of Brain Science.* New York, NY: Penguin Books.

Eldridge, L. L., S. A. Engel, M. M. Zeineh, S. Y. Bookheimer, and B. J. Knowlton, 2005, As cited in: Sousa, D. A. 2010. *Mind, Brain, & Education: Neuroscience Implications for the Classroom.* Bloomington, IN: Solution Tree.

Flavell, John H. 1979. "Metacognition and Cognitive Monitoring: A New Area of Cognitive-Developmental Inquiry." *American Psychologist,* 34: 906–911.

Harris, Bryan, and Cassandra Goldberg. 2012. *75 Quick and Easy Solutions to Common Classroom Disruptions.* Florence, KY: Routledge.

Huntington's Outreach Program for Education, at Stanford (HOPES). 2010. "Neuroplasticity." http://www.stanford.edu/group/hopes/cgi-bin/wordpress/2010/06/neuroplasticity.

Immordino-Yang, Mary H. and Matthias Faeth. 2010. "The Role of Emotion and Skilled Intuition in Learning." *Mind, Brain, and Education: Neuroscience Implications for the Classroom,* edited by David A. Sousa, 69–83. Bloomington, IN: Solution Tree.

Jensen, Eric. 2005. *Teaching with the Brain in Mind.* Alexandria, VA: Association for Supervision and Curriculum Development.

Medina, John. 2008. *Brain Rules: 12 Principles for Surviving and Thriving at Work, Home, and School.* Seattle, WA: Pear Press.

Merzenich, Michael. 2013. *Soft-Wired: How the New Science of Brain Plasticity Can Change Your Life.* San Francisco, CA: Parnassus Publishing, LLC.

Overbaugh, Richard C. and Lynn Schultz. n.d. *Bloom's taxonomy:* 22. Retrieved from http://ww2.odu.edu/educ/roverbau/Bloom/blooms_taxonomy.htm.